Praise fo

"This is the best site I have ever seen for prospective journalists."
—*Senior journalism major*

"I used the advice you give on the JobsPage Web site at just about every phase of my job hunt. I researched the paper (and the town I will be covering) online—which paid off big time when they asked me what I thought the major news stories in the area were. And the editors seemed impressed that I knew a handful of the writers on staff by name and beat.

"Oh, and of course I sent thank-you notes. Handwritten.

"Now that I have a job and don't have to compete against all my other unemployed or newly graduating journalism major friends, I will definitely pass them the link to the site."
—*Reporter*

"I met you years ago when you visited the University of Maryland, and you left a very positive impression. A few weeks ago, I stumbled across your JobsPage purely by chance. It's remarkable—I stayed several hours after work one night to read it over. I wish I had known about it earlier. Thanks for taking the time to put it together and making it accessible outside your own paper."
—*Reporter*

"I've been using JobsPage as a reference for about two years now. It's a great information resource that I've used when job-hunting and in educating myself on the real-life practices of the journalism world."
—*Student*

"I have just spent the last four hours browsing, reading and taking notes. What a great resource! I wish I had found it sooner."
—*Television journalist switching to print*

"I would just like to tell you how helpful your articles on job tips have been to me."
—*Magazine job hunter*

"I just called to thank you for your work on the JobsPage site for the Detroit Free Press. It's totally awesome and it's been totally helpful in the past couple weeks as I've been trying to get a job. There's so much information there. I never knew how to put my résumé together for a journalism job. Résumé books and so forth are almost useless for our line of work. They help me get pointers, but it's great to have a site break it down for journalists." —*Photographer*

"I'm a senior journalism major at Emerson College, but by the new year I will be working at my first official newspaper job, as a town reporter for the Cape Cod Times. And I have you (at least in part) to thank." —*Reporter*

"Your tips on the JobsPage Web site were priceless when I was making my career switch from attorney to journalist a couple years ago. It's the best job-hunting Web site for new journalists on the 'net.'"

"I wrote to you once about nine years ago about whether I should leave a daily newspaper to go to a start-up Web site or the AP. I contacted you again about six years ago to thank you for the advice. Luckily, I followed it and went to the wire. The Web site went out of business.

"I wanted to update you again to assure you that your advice has continued to pay off for me.

"From the wire service in Philadelphia, I went to the Inquirer. I had a good five-year run there, but left five months ago with the threat of layoffs looming.

"Now, I'm very happy at the Daily News in New York.

"I just wanted to thank you again for your help. The wrong move could have been disastrous." —*Reporter*

"For years I have been telling others what a great job you do with the jobs page so I thought I'd take a minute to tell you. As a professional journalist for years, I often pointed interns to your site. Now, I am teaching at Texas State University, and I use your site in class.

"What a great collection of information you offer. I've told several of your colleagues when we've run into each other at conferences, but I've just never told you. So now my mind is at ease. You're doing a great job, and I'll keep referencing your page in my classes.

"Thanks for taking the time to offer great advice to young journalists." —*Lecturer/print sequence coordinator*

JOE GRIMM
Breaking In

The JobsPage.com Guide
to Newspaper Internships

www.JobsPage.com

Some proceeds will go to journalism scholarships in memory of Detroit Free Press *Executive Editor Robert G. McGruder, 1942-2002*

"Please know that I stand for diversity. I represent diversity. I am the messenger and the message of diversity. I represent the African Americans, Latinos, Arab Americans, Asians, Native Americans, gays and lesbians, women, and all the others we must see represented in our business offices, newsrooms and our newspapers if we truly want to meet the challenge of serving our communities."

© 2008 by Joe Grimm. All rights reserved.
978-1-934879-03-0
Manufactured in the United States of America.

contents

how this guide was born

After I began recruiting for the *Detroit Free Press* in 1990, I noticed that some questions come up over and over again. It seemed that we newspaper editors do not explain ourselves very well. After hearing similar questions from so many people, I felt there must be others with the same concerns who could not ask me personally. So, I decided to put some answers online.

The JobsPage has always tried to be an honest and encouraging guide to newspaper careers. Today, with the newspaper industry in transition to more and more online news, that kind of help is more important than ever.

When the JobsPage was launched at the National Association of Hispanic Journalists convention in 1997, it was aimed at beginners. They had more questions and were more comfortable with the Web. The JobsPage has grown up with its early users, adding articles and answers for people well beyond the start of their careers.

Another convention prompted this book when, at the 2003 meeting of the National Association of Black Journalists, a student exclaimed, "I love the JobsPage so much I've printed out the whole thing. In fact, it broke my printer."

So many people have said they printed out stacks of JobsPage articles that we decided to make this book as a convenient carry-along for internship seekers.

This little book contains just part of the Web site. When we decided to publish the book, we filled in some of the blanks and added strategies that went only to people getting ready for *Free Press* internships. We hope this book and the additions it prompted for the Web site have made the JobsPage more helpful than ever.

"Breaking In" has been helped immeasurably by the copy editing of *Detroit Free Press* copy editor Emiliana Sandoval, the cover by *Free Press* artist Rick Nease, who has been with the JobsPage from the very beginning, and the design work of Maya Rhodes of Wayne State University Press. I'd also like to thank my industry colleagues who contributed their advice to "Breaking In."

Thanks to you, if you're one of the hundreds of curious, hopeful people whose questions helped build the JobsPage. You are the people that the JobsPage and "Breaking In" are for and by. I am happy about your interest in journalism and hope this book helps. I invite you to e-mail your ideas and questions to me at joe@newsrecruiter.com. I'll try to write back.

For me, there has been no greater reward and privilege than to help people achieve their dreams.

JOE GRIMM
Detroit Free Press
2007

features of "breaking in"

Guests
Several recruiters, editors, and journalists have generously let us include their advice in "Breaking In." We thank them and hope you get the chance to thank them, too. Their contributions are one of the best things about this book.

The Edge
The Edge was born when Wayne State University journalism student Val Hickey, on a visit to the *Detroit Free Press,* said, "The JobsPage is my edge." When she said that, a light went on and we started adding quick tips to the edges of JobsPage articles online. You'll find some on these pages, too, though we put them at the bottom of the pages.

Quotes
Nothing cuts to the quick like a quote. Many of the quotes in here come from "Today's Word on Journalism," collected by Edward C. Pease, Ph.D., professor and head of the Department if Journalism and Communication at Utah State University. Get on his e-mail list of snappy quotes by writing him at tpease@cc.usu.edu. More came from Tulsa World General Editor Rusty Lang and John McIntyre, assistant managing editor of the copy desk at the Baltimore Sun.

JobsPage in My Pocket
We made this book to bring you a portable JobsPage; we boiled some of our tips down to business-card size to make them even more portable. "JobsPage in My Pocket" tip tickets can be cut out or, if you'd rather not cut up your book, photocopied for pocket or purse. "JobsPage in My Pocket" cards are designed so that you'll have strategies with you for dealing with specific situations you might be anticipating.

1

Internships Launch Careers

Why internships are critical

Get an internship.

Get an internship.

Get an internship.

Get it?

There is not another thing you can do, short of buying your own newspaper and hiring yourself, that can do more to launch your career.

An internship is better for your career than spending the summer as campus editor or taking classes.

An internship is better for your career than backpacking through Europe.

An internship may not be better than staying close to Boyfriend or Girlfriend for the summer, but it is better for your career.

It is not easy to get a good internship. It takes an armload of work, a handful of planning and a pinch of luck. This book will help with all of that—maybe even the luck.

Internships, like nothing else, will do this for you:

- Show you what newspaper work is really like.
- Give you experience AND the published clips you'll need to get a job.
- Bring you the contacts, mentors, guides, and references to help you get jobs.

They might even let you use journalism to make money.

Internships have become on-ramps for newspaper jobs. Some of the biggest papers expect you to have internships just to get their internships.

Having one internship or more on your résumé can help you make the cut when others don't. But what if you never get an internship? Is your career over before it has even had a chance to start?

Of course not.

I never had an internship. And I got in. Of course, I entered journalism during the Paleolithic Era, when it was less important to have an internship than it was to know how to use stone tools. And I didn't have the JobsPage telling me what to do. If I had, I could have saved myself some trouble.

So, make it easy on yourself and get going.

Apply early

When should you apply? Right now! Immediately! Snap this book shut and hop onto your computer or phone!

Most qualified people who miss out on newspaper internships simply wait too long. Some wait way too long. I get calls and e-mails in late May from people who want to know whether we will be accepting any interns for the summer. Here's part of an e-mail I received one Memorial Day:

"Hi . . . I'm a photography major in New York. I'm home for the summer and was looking for a photo related job and/or internship. Just when I thought I was out of luck, I found your ad online. I was wondering if the internship position was filled. I honestly hope not. It sounds like the perfect opportunity for me. I have a portfolio and résumé all ready to go, and I can get three letters of interest within the next week or so. Hopefully I will hear from you soon, because I would love this opportunity."

Here is part of my response:

"Our photo internship was filled in January and the photo intern gets to town on Wednesday. I'm sorry.

"For the future, you should know that summer internships are typically filled months before summer ever gets here."

The time to apply for summer internships (do not adjust your eyeballs) is October and November.

That's right, for summer. If you haven't gotten your applications rolling by late November, there will be two turkeys at Thanksgiving—the one on the platter and you.

Some newspapers have humane deadlines as late as February or March. But the biggest papers close application windows by December 1 or earlier. Although I have seen offers as early as August, the first ones typically start dropping in October and November.

Get your apps out early to be in the mix.

Fall, winter, and spring internships are rare, so ask before you assume they exist. Generally, deadlines for non-summer internships are not as far in advance because the candidate pool is much smaller. While it can be difficult to find non-summer internships, the lack of competition for the ones you do find can be to your advantage. One strategy is to adjust your school year to take classes in the summer or to or delay graduation to have a shot at one of these off-summer internships. Just be sure you know where to apply—and what your chances are—before you rearrange your life.

Applying early also means not waiting until your last year of college to get an internship. One of the great things about a newspaper career is that you can begin now. Like, today. You don't have to wait until you earn your degree, become certified, get a license or pass your boards. Brain surgeons? They should wait. Journalists? We can start operating right away.

People start journalism even before they start college. And the people who start their careers earliest often are the ones who see them take off fastest.

Now that we have you all jazzed up to send your applications before you go to sleep tonight, we'll temper that advice. Know that application deadlines are probably earlier than you think and meet them, but send yours two to six weeks before the deadline. If you send your application months in advance, it might get misplaced. As in lost.

The Edge ——————————————————————————

Each year, the American Society of Newspaper Editors collects and posts information on newspaper internships across the country. The list can be especially helpful to people who are late in their internship searches because it includes application deadlines. It is at www.asne.org.

Guest: Amazing change in an amazing age

By BOBBI BOWMAN
Diversity Director
American Society of Newspaper Editors

You who are about to enter newsrooms will cover the biggest story of our lives—how the country turns from white to brown.

It's the story many of you grew up with in your schools and your colleges.

Preparing yourself to cover this amazing and historic story will make you a better journalist, a more accurate journalist and therefore better able to get a job and be an asset to the paper that hires you.

The story of how the USA turns from a majority white nation to a majority minority nation will change the politics, the economy, the social fabric, and democracy by mid-century. No country in its history has EVER undergone a change like this. You'll get to report on it and decide how to cover it.

When you look at a white baby, you are looking at the face of the new minority in the United States.

Why is the country changing so rapidly from California to Massachusetts? Immigration.

At the turn of the 20th Century, the Europeans came. If you are Polish, Italian, Greek, or Jewish, your great-great grandmother and grandfather came to this country in the late 1890's and early 1900's. They changed the face of the Northeast and the Midwest.

Now, in the infant years of the 21st century, it's the Mexicans, the Chinese, the Filipinos, the Koreans, the Indians who are coming. These

Bobbi Bowman is diversity director of the American Society of Newspaper Editors. Bowman began her career at The Washington Post as a suburban reporter and became an assistant city editor. She has also worked at the Detroit Free Press as deputy city editor, USA TODAY covering state and local politics, Gannett corporate offices, and as the managing editor of the Observer-Dispatch, a Gannett newspaper in Utica, New York. In March 1999, Bowman came to ASNE. She is a student of World War II and the 8th Air Force. In 2004, she stood on Omaha Beach with the heroes for the 60th anniversary of D-Day.

are the people, who, along with black Americans, this country has traditionally discriminated against.

Today, non-Hispanic whites make up 68 percent of the country's population, according to the U.S. Census Bureau. That number is falling.

Why should you care? It's about accuracy and fairness. Can a largely white staff cover a community that looks like a rainbow? Can a staff of 50-year-olds fairly cover a community of 20-somethings? The answer is yes—but.

The coverage is better if the reporting and editing staff brings a special knowledge insight into the culture, the history, and the roots of the community.

Certainly you can cover baseball without having played the game. But doesn't it help if you know about Mark McGwire, and Sammy Sosa, Babe Ruth, Hank Aaron, Jackie Robinson, Joe DiMaggio, the New York Yankees, the Brooklyn Dodgers, and the magic of Cooperstown? It's the difference between writing and writing with depth, context, perception, and accuracy.

You can cover Mexicans who are now Americans and do not speak Spanish. But doesn't it help if you can understand their life stories in their own language? For example, the way you say, "give birth to" in Spanish is to say "give light to." That's a different way of looking at the world.

Demographics is destiny. If you want to see the future, visit elementary schools in your community.

The impact of the demographic changes now washing over the country will be the best story going this century. What do you do to get ready?

- Learn to speak a foreign language. Arabic, Spanish, Urdu.
- If you are a minority, newspapers need you. Learn to report and write well.
- Learn to get along with people different from you. Go to a bat mitzvah. Go to a Polish-American celebration and dance a polka. Learn why the Ganges River is sacred to Hindus.
- Go to a NASCAR race.
- Be curious about everything.

Then you'll be ready to write the first draft of history for one of this nation's most amazing centuries. ✳

Be ready to move

Another reason good people miss out on internships is that they lack geographic imagination.

Let me illustrate. Two students at the University of Missouri-Columbia, a top journalism program, applied for internships. The first was an international student in the graduate program. She had a degree from a university in London and a thick pack of well-written magazine articles. She was impressive. She had focused her search on the popular area around San Francisco. Another student, a junior undergrad, had a few clips from the campus paper. They were OK. Knowing she had a lot of competition, she applied to a lot of papers in out-of-the-way places. One was the *Grand Forks Herald* in North Dakota.

I think you know how the story turned out. Because she applied to off-the-path newspapers, the junior overtook the international master's student in experience.

One student told me she planned to work in either Alabama or Michigan. Her rationale was that her parents lived in one place and an uncle lived in the other. That is no way to launch a newspaper career. Have faith in your ability to find a place to live—even in cities where you don't have any uncles.

Don't let location be a barrier; use it as a tool for breaking in. There are enough barriers already. If you worry first about where you'll stay, you'll stymie your chances for landing an internship in the first place. Student journalists who insist on looking only in cities where they have relatives or friends with spare couches won't be asking sources questions. They'll be asking customers, "Do you want fries with that?"

First internships

Expect to start small. If you want to work at a large newspaper, plan to wait your turn and work a plan that will take you there. Even if every

The Edge ———————————————————————————
Leslie Guevarra, deputy managing editor at the *San Francisco Chronicle*, has told people looking to crack into journalism to look for work in places that are really, really hot or really, really cold.

one of your professors tells you how incredibly gifted you are, there will be other candidates from other universities whose gifts appear to be equal and whose experience you must exceed. You must balance patience and ambition.

One summer, a couple of grad students took internships in Duluth, Minnesota, where they found wide-open opportunities for their writing and photography that likely would not have occurred at very many large newspapers. Each was able to do a major project. Those catapulted them ahead of their peers. One treated her summer as she would treat any adventure in a new and unfamiliar place. She launched her career and had a great time.

First experiences might not even be called internships. They might be called externships, apprenticeships, or co-ops. They might not have a formal name at all. The job title is not important. Just get experience in a professional setting. You'll be able to explain that on a résumé or in an interview.

Get the best experience you can, but be flexible as you get started. If you want to do news but can get only sports, sign up. If you want to take pictures and they want you to file pictures, do it. The secret is to get in the door. Once inside, show them you know how to work, do your assignment, learn everything you can and try to expand your role by being eager, helpful, and available. While the first job may not be ideal, it will become the experience that puts you on your career path.

Get out there and get working.

The Edge

Newspapers don't talk about them, but there are such things as subsidized internships. They work like this: The student attracts partial funding for an internship. It could be an award that will pay for working an internship or it could be a subsidy from the school. The inventive internship candidate tells the newspaper and says, "Look, I have a $3,000 stipend that will pay me to do an internship. Can I do it at your newspaper?" Several times, the *Detroit Free Press* has taken a subsidy and added to it to bring the intern up to standard internship pay. In fact, some of our best interns came to us this way.

Unpaid internships

Some newspapers—and a whole lot of television stations and magazines—offer unpaid internships. Why?

Because experience is so important that employers can get away with offering it without money. There are always people who will work just for the experience. Of course, unpaid internships favor people whose families have money. While we question media companies that do not pay people, we have to respect people who will work for free if they must.

Some journalists wonder whether an unpaid internship has the same prestige as one that is paid. And some journalists advise up-and-comers against taking them. While it seems you should get points for working for free, you just won't. It all comes down to results. The fact that a newspaper does not pay you implies that you did not meet the same standards as people who draw paychecks. After all, the newspaper that does not pay its interns has less invested in them. You want to be so good they feel either ashamed or sly that they're not paying you. The whole point of working so hard on an unpaid internship is to make damn sure it will be the last time you ever have to work for free. While the lack of a paycheck demonstrates a lower commitment on the part of the paper, future editors generally judge the quality of applicants' internships by the kind of work they did rather than by whether—or how much—they were paid. Few hiring editors ever ask candidates how much they were paid in their previous internships. Your résumé should not say whether you were paid, either.

Try hard to get a paid internship for the obvious reason and because monetary investment is often followed by the more important investments of mentoring and editing.

Failure to land an internship means you'll likely pay for it later by starting at a smaller paper or for less money.

Don't let the money on internships distract you. These are not, after all, your money years. The prize here, my friends, is experience. It would be a mistake to pass up an opportunity to work in a newsroom for something that pays better but does not give you any journalistic experience. This shortsightedness could cost you money—and soon.

Let's imagine that Kyle and Terry both want to be newspaper reporters and are equally qualified.

Kyle takes an internship at a newspaper that pays just $1,000 for the summer.

Terry, mindful of tuition bills, takes a factory job instead because it pays $5,000.

Terry is ahead by $4,000.

They graduate and both get newspaper jobs. But, because of that internship experience, Kyle starts at $25,000. Terry, who had no internship, starts at $21,000 a year. By the end of their first year, they are even on money, even given Terry's high-paying factory job.

But it doesn't stop there.

They do equally well as reporters and each earns a five-percent raise. Kyle is now making $26,250 a year and Terry gets a raise to $22,050. By the end of their second year, Kyle has now earned $4,200 more than Terry. And the wage disparity is growing

Let's give them each another five-percent raise for their third year. Kyle moves to $27,562.50 and Terry moves up to $23,152.50. Terry's salary is still not where Kyle started—that will take two more years of five-percent raises. Terry, who took the lucrative factory job while Kyle was eating macaroni and cheese, is $8,610 behind after their third year, even taking their internship summer into account. Terry's factory job paid more, but Kyle's experience has been worth a whole lot more.

Getting a newspaper career to take off starts with a succession of steps. If an unpaid internship is the only way to get professional experience and you can find a way to afford it, do it.

One who did: A college senior applied for an internship at the *Detroit Free Press* using clips from a suburban newspaper where she had worked the summer before. We knew that the other newspaper seldom paid interns. She confirmed she had worked for free. "I am paying for most of my college and really need to earn money, so I worked for the paper free three days a week, and had another job, outside of journalism, for about five days a week." Her strategy proved she could work; her clips proved she could write. The *Free Press* gave her a paid internship and, at the end of the internship, offered her a permanent job. She would not have landed the internship or the job if she had not found a way to generate the clips that got her in the door.

If you're going to work for low pay or no pay, you have the right to ask for as much opportunity as you can get. Ask for it even if they *are* paying you.

National internship programs

Most internships are offered by individual newspapers. Some papers belong to groups or chains, like Gannett and McClatchy, that have recruiters who help more than one paper. But you will almost always be dealing with newspapers one at a time. Two large, national internship programs are exceptions.

Chips Quinn Scholars program

This program, which started with six scholars in 1991, now finds internships for about seventy-five journalists of color every year. Its alumni claim more than two-hundred forty colleges. The program was established in the memory of John "Chips" Quinn Jr., editor of the *Poughkeepsie Journal,* who died at age thirty-four and who was committed to increasing newsroom diversity. The Freedom Forum administers the program.

The program offers training and mentoring in addition to internship placement. Chips Quinn interns can work in reporting, photography, copy editing, design and online. Internships are offered in spring and summer and carry $1,000 scholarships.

Two aspects of the program merit special note:

- It can be an entry point for candidates coming from colleges overlooked by full-time recruiters.
- The mentoring and networking that come with Chips Quinn internships are powerful.

The Edge _____

Read about the program that has launched more than a thousand careers at www.chipsquinn.org/. You'll see how the program was founded, who has come into it and how they keep things growing. The contact information is:

Chips Quinn Scholars
Freedom Forum
1101 Wilson Blvd.
Arlington, VA 22209
(703) 284-3934

Dow Jones Newspaper Fund internships

The Dow Jones Newspaper Fund is the nation's largest internship program. The Dow Jones Newspaper Fund is a foundation that encourages careers in journalism. It runs several programs for high school students, college students and teachers. Programs of particular interest to college journalists offer internships in two high-demand areas: copy editing and business reporting. The Dow Jones Newspaper Fund has been training copy editors for decades, and the program has earned a solid-gold reputation with newspapers. Some perks of being a Dow Jones intern:

- Great training
- All the internships are paid
- A $1,000 scholarship if you're returning to school
- Transportation to the training centers and to your internship
- That solid-gold résumé credential

Learn more about the programs—and find out how to apply—on the Dow Jones Newspaper Fund Web sites.

Guest: Consider copy editing

By RICH HOLDEN
Executive Director
Dow Jones Newspaper Fund

We've all seen the telltale signs:

- Reading a restaurant menu not for the food but to find typographical errors;
- Engaging in late-night discussions about the pluperfect participial;
- Checking the bowling agate to make sure the totals are correct;
- Agreeing that you're anal retentive but willing to argue about whether it should be hyphenated.

The Edge ————————————————————————————————
Read about and apply for the various programs that the Dow Jones Newspaper Fund offers at http:djnewspaperfund.dowjones.com/fund/.

If you're guilty of the above, the chances are that you're a copy editor or that you would make a good one. And in today's work environment, good editors are as much in demand as ever.

Some things haven't changed much over the years, and I'll offer one personal example on that point. In 1973 I visited the Chicago bureau of *The Wall Street Journal*, which was interested in hiring me as a commodities reporter. I mentioned to the bureau chief that I really was much more interested in editing than I was in reporting.

The reaction was immediate: a call by the bureau chief to the *Journal*'s managing editor in New York, a roundtrip plane ticket, a hotel room for a week and a copy of the paper's stylebook. Within a week I was in New York, had a tryout and was offered a job on the national desk, which I eagerly accepted.

More than thirty years later, I'm still with Dow Jones (the publisher of the *Journal*) and still very interested in and committed to finding talented young copy editors. Every December, I and a group of college professors have the delightful job of selecting more than 100 college students for editing internships at newspapers around the country.

It's interesting to note that even when newspapers go through difficult economic times, they remain firm in their desire to find copy editors through the Dow Jones Newspaper Fund. And I am positive that this interest will remain strong in the future.

I'm often asked what makes a good copy editor. I think it takes three elements—a love of the language, an inquisitive mind, and an ability to work well with others.

A love of the language is more than memorizing the Associated Press stylebook or knowing the difference between further and farther or compose and comprise (yes, I still have to look them up). It's being

Rich Holden has been executive director of the Dow Jones Newspaper Fund since 1992. Prior to that, he was an editor for twenty years at The Wall Street Journal in New York and Hong Kong.

able to retain a reporter's "voice" when trimming a twenty-inch story to fifteen inches, and it's being able to come up with creative headlines that don't mimic a reporter's lead paragraph. And, yes, it is knowing when to use the subjunctive mood and when to use the indicative.

Good editors are curious by nature. They know what questions to ask a reporter and when to ask them. They know that what may seem like an important question two hours before deadline may not be so important fifteen minutes before deadline. And they know the difference between simply wanting to know more about a particular topic and straightening out a matter of fairness or libel in copy.

Finally, a good editor is a good co-worker. It may sound trite, but a copy desk really is a team. If you can't work well with others, often under a good deal of pressure, perhaps you should consider air-conditioning repair or over-the-road trucking. The last question I would ask myself before hiring a copy editor was: "If the roles were reversed, would I feel comfortable working for this person?" If I couldn't answer "yes," that person wasn't hired.

So, if you meet these criteria, editing could be for you. The biggest mistake college students make is writing off some aspect of the newspaper business before they ever try it. Too many want to be reporters, and reporters only, when many jobs in editing go begging. A good editor is never going to be an unemployed editor. The same can't be said for reporters.

And, when people ask me what's the best thing about being an editor, I have a simple answer. It's much more fun being the arrow than it is the target. ✴

Tweeners: Between internships and jobs

In between newspaper internships and permanent jobs are the "tweeners."

They've proliferated to the point where some new grads and even pros look specifically for these fixed-term, post-graduate jobs.

Tweeners come in many flavors. They range in length from six months to three years. At the *Chicago Tribune* and *Providence Journal,* it's two years. At the *Seattle Times,* it's three. The *Newark Star-Ledger* has a one-year program.

They come with different names, too. At the *Tribune,* they are called residencies. In Seattle, they are still called internships, even after some-one has worked on staff for three years. At the *Star Ledger,* they are internships.

Some outfits, like the Associated Press, offer internships with the promise of a likely job at the end. Most tweeners, however, come with an expiration date and no promise of even a good-bye cake. Still, they give you more than a three-month internship would, and can be good if you're out of school or have already worked a couple of internships.

The sunset dates put tweeners in a niche by themselves. A *Wall Street Journal* article said, "Some of America's big metropolitan newspapers have discovered what corporate America found out long ago: They can cut costs by hiring temporary labor for high-profile newsroom jobs such as reporters and photographers. . . . Turning entry-level jobs into temporary positions alarms industry observers, who accuse newspa-pers of . . . contributing to a decline in full-time jobs with full benefits." The article was written by an intern.

At their best, tweeners help you get in the door at newspapers that would want more experienced candidates. The bar is lower for tween-ers than it is for jobs. At some papers, certain positions are reserved for tweeners. A one-year program at a larger paper might get you better editing, better experience and more money than you would otherwise find in your first job. Many first jobs last just a year or two anyway, so you might be further ahead with the larger paper's tweener than with a small paper's job.

But, beware. At their worst, tweeners can leave you feeling exploit-ed. Many tweener hires are paid at cut rates, even though their work may be the same as what other staffers are doing for full price. Some omit health insurance.

It's hard to not feel second-best when the newspaper's commitment is temporary and the pay is lower. Minority journalists, who get a dis-proportionate share of these short-term offers at some papers, wonder why they aren't getting the permanent jobs. At one paper, some staffers have referred to people on two-year arrangements as "Bics"—like the throwaway pens. Ask about such things before you accept and be sure to talk to people who have been through the program.

In some cases, ballyhooed "programs" turn out to be nothing but hooey.

Cruelest of all are the cases where journalists quit permanent jobs to take tweeners and talk themselves into believing that, in the spirit of Horatio Alger, they'll be the exceptions who make it and get asked to stay on. When that doesn't happen, they feel cheated—and unemployed.

So, protect yourself. Know the traps and the tricks, and use these fixed-term programs to start your career or kick it into a higher orbit. Look for those that really do offer training that you can't get in any other way and that will help you get your next job. MetPro, run by the Tribune Company, has had a good success record. So has Hearst's rotating internship program. There are plenty of people working in newspapers today who owe some of their success to what they learned in those tweeners.

The secret is to know exactly what you're getting into and to evaluate these opportunities in light of your career plans.

Guest: **Business reporting has your number**

By CATHY PANAGOULIAS
Assistant Managing Editor
The Wall Street Journal

If you hope to be an investigative reporter, a great feature writer or a knowledgeable beat reporter, business reporting is for you. Yes, business reporting.

Sure, you'll have to learn what a stock is, but rest assured most people don't go into business reporting knowing much about either the stock market or numbers.

JobsPage in My Pocket: What to ask about tweeners.

If you get an offer, in addition to the usual questions about salary and benefits, you should ask these questions when considering an extended internship:

- Is this a training program?
- If so, what kind of training is provided?
- What training opportunities does the newspaper provide to staff in general?
- How many people are hired out of this program?
- Where do the others go?
- When does the newspaper recommend I start the search for a permanent job?
- Will the newspaper help me in my next job hunt? How?

If you have good basic skills, you can learn the jargon and develop the knowledge to cover a variety of beats in a variety of media. And, you can do groundbreaking stories that make a difference.

Most major newspapers have business pages, and the larger ones like *The Washington Post* have a section. *The Wall Street Journal* is all about business. Then there are the magazines—*Forbes, Fortune,* and *Business Week.* But a huge chunk of the business press works for wire services. The biggest are Bloomberg, Reuters and Dow Jones Newswires, which is part of the company that owns the *Journal.* Then there is television. Bloomberg and CNBC and others are now offering business news. Dozens of Web sites have sprouted up, from The Street.com to CNET, which focus on technology. Beyond that, there are literally hundreds of magazines and newsletters devoted to business reporting. So the bottom line here is there are lots of jobs and a wide range of jobs in the business press.

Business reporting today includes coverage of the stock market and anything having to do with companies. Basically, any time money is being spent, there's a business story somewhere. And for every topic, there's a business angle. Computer viruses, cell-phone price wars, fashion trends, entertainment, Nike commercials, fast-food menus, and health-care costs all have been subjects of business stories.

Business topics have lent themselves to both great investigative reporting and remarkable feature writing. In business, we cover many things that readers can identify with; we just do so in a special way. We follow the money. So instead of writing a hand-wringing story about children shooting children with cheap guns, we trace the gun used in one such killing and tell readers how a couple of small companies are importing these guns and selling them on the street. That kind of reporting changes gun laws.

Cathy Panagoulias is an assistant managing editor at *The Wall Street Journal, where she focuses on recruiting, hiring, and the intern program. From 1995 to 2000 she ran the Journal's news desk, responsible for all breaking news. Previously she was the technology editor, and before that held a range of editing and management jobs in New York and Hong Kong.*

So, how do you become a business reporter? Several different paths can all lead to success.

You can start at a small newspaper, move on to a bigger paper as you switch beats and eventually land at either a major paper or business magazine. You don't have to cover business in all your beats, but it's not a bad idea to develop some expertise in an area that involves some industries. Transportation, environmental issues, education, health care, and food are areas that could be useful. Other people start at a Web site and move to a wire service or print.

You can have a fabulous career at wire services partly because all the wires have huge overseas staffs. If you want to work overseas, start learning a language, particularly if you are still in college. Arabic, Chinese, Japanese, German, and French are all sought after. If you are a good reporter and have a language, you can jump to the head of the line in many instances. Spanish is extremely useful at any U.S. publication, and there is a growing Hispanic media in this country that needs more reporters who can write and report in Spanish.

Another common path is to start at a trade publication. Every industry has publications devoted to it. During the tech boom, dozens and dozens of tech magazines and weekly newspapers were devoted to every possible part of the industry. If you start at such a place, whether the focus is technology or Hollywood or restaurants, you will soon have a contact list of many industry experts, and that list is a selling point in getting your next job. If a newspaper, for example, is looking for someone to cover the fast-food industry and you just earned your spurs at Burger Business Weekly, you'll get an interview. The main drawback here is that some publications are so narrow that it is hard to see how well rounded you are from evaluating such clips. So you have to find a way to compensate for focus by including clips that show range.

In the end, there is no single formula for success. As long as you learn your craft and are devoted to it, you will find a way to get a great job in business reporting. ✳

Late bloomers

Not all of us have the good fortune to know in sixth grade what we want to be when we grow up. And, we have become a nation of career-changers. Newspaper journalism can be a second or third career. If you're a late-bloomer or a career-changer, can internships be part of your strategy?

Not very often.

Although students who do not pursue internships until senior year will likely get something better than the inexperienced sophomores, they will be outdone by other seniors who started interning as sopho-mores.

Late-bloomers, just like early-bloomers, will likely have to start small. The difficulty is that late-blooming college students or career-switchers may not have the flexibility to push through a series of in-ternships and jobs to get to the ones that pay well. Career-switchers especially can get grouchy if editors do not give much consideration to their non-journalism experience. While the wise newspaper editor may be the one who spots journalistic talent in non-journalistic work histories, it is the wise job-seeker who uses résumé and interview to point out those qualities.

Those who have been out of school for several months may find that editors feel they are beyond the internship window. Editors figure that candidates who have not had any professional experience by the time they are several months beyond graduation lack not just experi-ence, but perhaps commitment. They see red flags.

Career-switchers can rarely afford to quit permanent jobs for ten- or twelve-week gigs. Knowing that, editors are reluctant to ask them to. They do not want to entice a person out of a real job, only to see that person try desperately and unsuccessfully to parlay an internship into something permanent.

If you're in one of these groups, other options are to freelance to the point where you can get hired into a permanent newspaper job or go to graduate school, which will put you back into the internship field. We'll have more on both of those avenues later.

Guest: **Mid-career entry points**

By WANDA LLOYD
Executive Editor
Montgomery Advertiser

If you are a mature adult (say, over the age of twenty-five), a talented writer, Web content provider, photographer, videographer, or graphic artist with good grammar and critical thinking skills, the newspaper industry may be looking for you.

No longer the entry-level bastion for young people with brand-new journalism school degrees, some newspaper editors now recognize the benefits of finding mid-career professionals who may be contemplating a career change—people who are military retirees, law enforcement officers, teachers, social workers, accountants, broadcasters, administrators, public relations specialists, or any number of professionals.

The Freedom Forum Diversity Institute (www.diversityinstitute. org) in Nashville in 2002 developed a model for helping newspapers identify and train mid-career people of color for professional newsroom positions. Diversity Institute fellows were nominated by their local newspaper companies, sent to the Institute's intensive twelve-week training program and returned home as professional journalists to work for their local daily newspaper.

Because of this program and a changing workforce climate that has editors seeking solutions for creative staffing and career development, this may be a good time for mid-career professionals of any race or background to seek an opportunity in journalism.

Here are some tips for developing a plan to transition into daily newspaper journalism.

- Take a couple of journalism classes at a community college. If nothing else, the courses might give you a clearer picture of whether this is the direction you want to take.
- If you work in a major metropolitan area, start your search at a small- or medium-size newspaper. Large metro newspapers generally do not hire entry-level candidates. For those that are the exception, there are plenty of recent journalism school graduates with one, two or more daily newspaper internships. It's unlikely you will beat those odds.
- Begin your career-change search in your own backyard. Editors

Wanda Lloyd, executive editor of the Montgomery Advertiser in Alabama, was the founding executive director of the Freedom Forum Diversity Institute at Vanderbilt University. She is a recipient of the Ida B. Wells Award for media diversity. In 2007, she won a Robert G. McGrudee Award for Diversity Leadership.

often value a local person's knowledge of the community and the contacts that knowledge will bring. For what you can bring to the table, an editor may be willing to provide the training on the technical aspects of journalism.

- Unlike a few years ago, now tech experience counts. If you have skills with digital video or audio, if you know certain Web software programs or if you have been a television or radio professional, there may be a future for you in your local daily newspaper's newsroom.
- Be well-read. In making your pitch to an editor, be sure you have read that newspaper and the newspaper's Web site consistently and that you are able to converse on a sophisticated level about the organization's strengths and weaknesses relevant to how it covers the local community.
- Despite your years of experience in another field, consider that you will be seen as entry-level in journalism. Be prepared for the possibility of a reduced salary or working a schedule that may not look like bankers' hours.

Changing careers can be tough. Getting into journalism—often seen as a closed society only for people who have newsroom internships, work samples, and journalism degrees—can be daunting. If you are truly passionate about a newsroom career, don't give up if the first or second news organization turns you down. Keep looking for the ideal situation.

Ask each editor you meet for critical feedback about your application and your chances for success. Work on the deficient areas.

As John Quinn, former editor of *USA TODAY*, often tells new industry recruits, journalism is "the most fun you can have with your clothes on." ✷

Guest: Career-switcher came into photojournalism

By HARRY WALKER
Photo Service Director
McClatchy-Tribune News Service

Photojournalism can be an exciting, challenging, and rewarding profession. It offers challenges to your creativity, physical endurance, technical know-how, and organizational skills.

Where else can you be in a profession that challenges your creative talents while giving you the opportunity to educate yourself? Photography allows you to work with almost any subject you can think of, from business to technology to sports to politics to entertainment to . . .

Many photographers are constantly amazed at the opportunities presented to them—opportunities they more than likely would never experience in another profession.

For example, as director of the McClatchy-Tribune Photo Service, I witnessed most major sporting events and history-making political events and enjoyed tremendous access to entertainment venues. I have traveled to several countries as part of my job.

From working at a small-town newspaper to working at the White House, photographers are given the opportunity to experience interesting topics and people.

This is a profession where the sky literally is the limit. With talent, you can go as far and as fast as you like. The best part is that a degree from a college or journalism school is preferred, but not required. Your photos or portfolio are your key to success. You need only to take really good journalistic photos, have good people and organizational skills, understand technology, and be able to physically endure all the opportunities you will be exposed to. What a job.

A successful photographer will assemble a diverse portfolio. It should include photo stories, single images (sports, news, breaking news, features, illustrations), and photo illustrations. The portfolio should contain a diversity of ethnic subjects as well. This will demonstrate your ability to navigate your way through a variety of people and cultures and situations.

Harry Walker switched from a career in banking as a branch manager to move into photojournalism, working as a newspaper photographer and editor before becoming the director of McClatchy-Tribune, the second-largest wire photo service in the United States.

The most important aspect of being a successful photojournalist is to remember that you are a journalist. You report with photos instead of words. Your tool is a camera instead of a keyboard. Visual journalists are as important to the success of any publication as anyone else in the organization.

At McClatchy-Tribune, we work with many top photographers at local newspapers and offer them opportunities that are exciting and rewarding. We recruit photographers from local papers for stories of national and international interest: presidential campaigns, Super Bowls, Olympics, the aftermath of a suicide bombing in Israel, the war in Iraq. And these opportunities are available to all. Photographers have been chosen for national projects from papers in cities as small as Bradenton, Florida, and Macon, Georgia, as well as papers in metropolitan areas like Detroit, Miami, Philadelphia and San Jose.

I encourage anyone with a passion for photojournalism to pursue it. ✷

Too many internships

So-called professional interns who start right out of high school and wind up with four or five internships (the most I've ever seen has been ten) wonder whether there is such a thing as too many internships.

Yes, you can have too many.

It's not the number of internships that can hurt as much as how long you keep interning after you become job-eligible. You can work as many internships as you like while you're in college, but don't keep doing that after college.

If papers, even large ones, hire you for internships but not for jobs, editors at other newspapers might wonder why that is. After all, internships are, in a way, dress rehearsals. Editors may wonder if a lot of places are getting a look at how you work, but no one is trying to keep you.

Internships are short-term propositions. You show up, you work for three months, you leave. If you're not great, no one has to fire you. We just have to wait you out. So, hiring an intern is low-risk. Hiring a permanent staffer with minimal experience is high-risk. Editors are not big risk-takers. We never like to make hiring mistakes, not even on internships, so we hire conservatively. In internships, as in jobs, editors try to hire sure-fired, guaranteed, can't-miss successes. One of the best ways to hire a successful intern is to hire one who is pretty much an expert at being an intern. Conservative hiring makes editors eager to offer fifth internships, but cautious about flipping interns into first jobs.

There is one exception where multiple post-graduate internships are not a detriment: Hearst, Tribune Company and others bundle two or more internships into rotating programs. These run for a year or two and do not start until graduation for obvious reasons.

Your Directory:
The *Editor & Publisher International Year Book*

The number of journalism students who have not heard of the *Editor & Publisher International Year Book* stuns me. It is essential equipment in the internship and job hunt.

The *E&P Year Book* is a directory of all the daily and weekly newspapers in the United States and most of the dailies throughout North America and the rest of the world. Use *Editor & Publisher* to look up all the newspapers in an area, state or region, and to learn about them. The *E&P Year Book*, as it is known, will tell you the newspaper's circulation and owner, its address, and phone number, its Web site and who its key editors are. You can get a lot of this information on the Web, but you can find it faster with the *E&P Year Book*. Without it, you are walking through a forest at night without a flashlight.

The yearbook, which comes out annually, is expensive—well more than $100. But you can look at it for free in most journalism departments, newsrooms, and good career services departments. Do not expect it to be sitting out in the open where it might sprout legs. If you cannot get a look at it at school or at the newspaper, check with

The Edge ――――――――――――――――――――――――――――――

As newspapers have developed online products, so has Editor & Publisher. You can find some of the latest industry news at http://www.editorand-publisher.com. Another great site for that is Jim Romenesko's column on the Poynter Website at www.poynter.org. Many professionals make these part of their daily reading.

the reference desk at a good public library. If career services does not have a copy, suggest they start buying it every year as a resources for students.

One note of caution: Before writing to the editors in the book, call, e-mail or check the newspaper's Web site to be sure you have the name and title correct. There occasionally are mistakes in *E&P* and editors do change, so some of its entries become outdated even while it is on the press.

Editor & Publisher also has a monthly magazine by the same name about newspaper industry news.

Internship hunter's checklist

☐ List the papers to which you will apply. Include some stretch papers and some safety papers, just as you may have done when you applied for college. Apply for unpaid internships as a backup if you can afford to. Use the *Editor & Publisher Year Book* as a guide.

☐ Check application requirements and list the papers according to their deadlines.

☐ Get the addresses and names of the contact people by visiting Web sites or calling. You can get Web sites with a search engine, but save yourself some time by using a site that has collected all the links in one convenient place like the Newspaper Association of America's News-Voyager at http://www.newspaperlinks.com/voyager.cfm Note application requirements and deadlines.

☐ Tune up your résumé and cover letter. Have someone who is a good editor check it over closely. Do not ask your mother (who loves you), your best friend (who can't spell) or your professor (who has no time), but use someone good who will be thorough and critical.

☐ Get your clips together.

☐ Make sure you have written essays, if required.

☐ Mail everything two to six weeks ahead of the deadlines.

☐ Whenever possible, interview with editors on campus, at conventions, or at their newspapers.

The JobsPage internship calendar

Landing an internship is a year-round process, not a flurry of activity late one night in the winter. The biggest mistake people make is waiting too long to look for summer internships. The earliest deadlines are in early November for the next summer. This calendar tells you what you can do each month of the year to stay on top of the internship hunt.

Month	If you're still looking	If you have one
January	• Mail remaining applications. Check for application dates. • Write thank-you notes for winter-break interviews. • Start calling prime papers	• Celebrate! • Take the rest of the month off.
February	• Still no offers? Stay calm. A few deadlines remain. • Phone calls to your prime newspapers could help.	• Begin reading the paper regularly. • Identify staffers you want to meet. • Remember to read paper on-line.
March	• Begin trying weekly newspapers • Line up free-lance jobs with newspapers or magazines. • Volunteer as a journalist with a local non-profit.	• Ask for newspaper's stylebook and begin learning it. • Get maps and information from the chamber of commerce.
April	• Call your prime newspapers to see whether anything opened up unexpectedly.	• Arrange for housing. • Line up transportation.
May	• No internship and out of school? Look for another way to break in. • Available for an internship next summer? Free-lance to beef up portfolio.	• Try to arrive early to look around community. • Arm yourself with a list of story ideas.
June	• If you haven't lined up stringing work, set something up by visiting editors at local papers. Experience may be more important than the money.	• Request a mentor, or ask someone to mentor you.

Month	If you're still looking	If you have one
July	• Talk to papers you plan to apply to for the next summer. Visit, if you can.	• Work hard and ask for more. • Actively seek feedback, advice.
August	• Evaluate your portfolio. Make plans to give it what it needs by working in student publications and freelancing when school resumes.	• Ask for a written appraisal. • Line up references. • Seek advice on your next move.
September	• Get your résumé together. Have someone edit it before you send it anywhere. • Make sure your portfolio is up to date and tightly edited. • Decide where you want to apply, learn the deadlines, meet the application requirements. • Begin regular checks for campus interviews and postings at the journalism department and career center.	
October	• Mail your first applications. Earliest deadlines for summer internships are Nov. 1 and creeping earlier. • Do on-campus interviews—even if just for practice. Ask professors and editors for critiques. • Diversify and improve portfolio.	
November	• This is your busiest month for sending applications. Most deadlines are between November 15 and January 1.	
December	• Big month for internship offers. • Interview at a newsroom or two on winter break.	

JobsPage in My Pocket

Recruiters track top prospects for years. They keep track of where prospects are and they try to maintain regular contact. It's smart for internship- and job-seekers to do the same with the best people they meet during their searches. Get key information when you meet people and keep track of your contacts on paper, in your computer's address book or with a database.

Contact:
Title:
Company:
E-mail:
Business phone:
Cell phone:
Where we met:
Key piece of advice/lesson:
Subsequent meetings, phone calls, letters or e-mails:
Date for next contact:

2

Journalism School

Anyone who thinks about a career in newspapers quite naturally thinks about journalism school. Every state has at least one journalism program—some are quite good—and newspapers count on them to get students ready for the newsroom. Scores of newspapers make campus visits a regular part of their recruiting effort and many newspaper journalists teach in J-schools.

But a J-degree alone is not enough to get you off to a good start in newspapering, and experience on a campus paper is no substitute for working in a professional newsroom. Do not listen to people who tell you that excelling in school—or on the student paper—is sufficient. It just isn't. But these experiences can be a critical part of getting started, especially combined with the professional experience you can get on internships.

The key academic question in the mind of most student journalists is whether they must earn a journalism degree. The answer is no. A J-degree can help, and it can be fun, but it is not required.

Some aspects of journalism are best learned in the structured regimen of the classroom. Journalism law, ethics, and economics are better learned within an academic context, rather than on a case-by-case basis.

Reporting, writing, photography, editing, design, and graphics skills are mastered under real-world, deadline conditions—provided you have good editors. Even with the best editors, you may find that J-schools provide good beginning and systematic training that no newsroom will offer.

Besides giving you the foundation and the framework, the classroom can be a safe place to ask questions and to practice. Each complements the other.

A journalism degree tells editors that you're serious about the craft, it gives you confidence in the fundamentals and, for many, a J-degree lets you study the thing you're most passionate about.

But a journalism degree is neither a requirement nor the only thing you need.

Every year, many people who do not have journalism degrees get newspaper internships and jobs. Editors hire them because they have learned their journalism on the job at campus publications and during newsroom internships.

Some of the best universities in the country do not offer journalism degrees, but newspapers will hire from them, anyway. Some journalists don't come to journalism until after they have committed to another major or have graduated. And many journalists deliberately major in areas they could specialize in as journalists. Each path can work. Newsrooms hire people from all these perspectives because editors are interested in getting people who have a range of backgrounds.

Good majors for journalists include political science, history, languages, English (especially for copy editors), criminal justice, law, education, business, finance, technology, the arts, and sociology. Because so many journalists avoid math and the sciences, it's good to find the exceptional journalists who know something about those areas, too.

If you decide not to major in journalism, that's fine. Be prepared to answer editors who ask how your non-journalism major contributes to good newspapering. And take some classes about ethics and law.

One key advantage of attending a good journalism school is that it puts you into an environment where you must learn and compete with other good journalists. Seek out the best professors and students in the program. They will make you better. A good journalism program—really, its student body—attracts recruiting editors. J-schools typically arrange interviews only for students in the J-school. A good career services office in a J-school will be much more attuned to journalism careers than a plain-vanilla university-wide service.

If you are not in a journalism program and want to interview with newspapers, join a journalism association that holds conventions with job fairs—and get yourself to some of those conventions.

Accredited J-schools

This guide is really intended for journalists who are in college or beyond, not those who are choosing one, but sometimes a smart person will slip through the cracks and get the book early. What do we call those people? Eventually, we call them "Boss." For the benefit of you early achievers, here is one paragraph about journalism school accreditation:

The Accrediting Council on Education in Journalism and Mass Communication (ACEJMC) reviews journalism and mass communications programs. There are about a hundred accredited J-schools and even more journalism and communication programs that are not. What does accreditation mean? It means that a school has met the council's standards. Accreditation can make it easier to attract faculty, grants, and scholarships and all of that can help you. But this does not mean that non-accredited J-schools are a waste of your time or money. I recruit at accredited and non-accredited programs every year. Accreditation does not weigh into my selection criteria. I find that the student bodies overlap. The strong students in weaker programs are better than the weak students in stronger programs. Consider accreditation, but do not treat it as the deciding factor. And, wherever you go, work to be one of the best, Boss.

Campus experience is not enough

Some college newspaper editors insist that their papers are as good as or better than the local paper in their towns and that college experience should count as much as working at the local paper. To most of us editors, though, it simply does not measure up, no matter how great the college paper is. You may think we're wrong—and maybe we are—but this is the reality you're going to have to work with.

The Edge ──────────────────────────────────────

You can find out which journalism programs are accredited—and more about what that means—at http://www.ku.edu/~acejmc/. The list also has links to the Web sites for those programs.

Editors will almost always place a higher value on experience at mainstream newspapers—even lousy ones—than experience at college newspapers—even great ones—because mainstream newsrooms are simply more like our own newsrooms than college newspapers are.

The range in age and experience in a college newsroom is much narrower than it is in a mainstream newspaper. The newest person in a mainstream newsroom is almost always more experienced than the college paper veteran. The average workweek is shorter in a college newsroom. Examples abound of students who live at their college newspapers, trashing their grades, but they are at the bleeding edge. The average workweek for the staff at a mainstream newspaper is a lot closer to forty hours a week than it is for the overall staff at a college newspaper.

Dailies, even small ones, publish five, six or seven days a week. Good college newspapers seldom go five times a week year round. The fact that your college newspaper published just as frequently or has a larger circulation than the daily you're applying to just won't carry much weight.

The news diet is different at a campus paper, and it should be. While many college newspapers include city, national, or international news and even travel for stories, they typically focus on campus issues.

So, you see, while the quality of a college newspaper can be as high as that of a mainstream newspaper, editors put a higher value on experience that is more similar to what they themselves are doing.

Don't waste your time lamenting that collegiate experience doesn't get the respect you think it should. The value of your college experience will show up in all kinds of ways on the job. But it will not be judged equal to experience in a professional newsroom. So get some.

Academic internships

Universities do students a favor when they require them to work professional internships. But that is just the barest beginning. To really help their students' careers, universities should have professors who push and a career services staff that helps students land internship after internship after internship.

Don't leave your career up to career services. They can't do it all.

Students must be in charge of getting their internships, and cannot entrust their futures to anyone else. Internships are a personal responsibility. As an editor, I would not hire anyone who I knew made it a habit of asking career services, "What are you doing to find me a job?" That lack of ownership is a red flag. Figure out how career services can help you—and how it can help you more than it helps the other students—and use what it has. Do not waste time rating the quality of the department. Your effectiveness in using it matters a whole lot more than your opinion of it.

Students who achieve a minimal graduation requirement of a single internship may be in for a shock. One student came to me in tears after what had seemed to her to be a picture-perfect college career. She had earned good grades, she had worked a job that let her graduate debt-free and she had done an internship. One internship. It had been in public relations, not journalism, and the successful graduate found that no newspaper or television station felt she had the journalistic experience she needed to compete. Just as soon as she had earned her degree, she decided she needed to go back to school. She thought she was finished and she learned she had not really started. Get as much experience as you can. The one-internship requirement is good, but minimal.

I applaud colleges for kicking students out of the nest and into the newsroom, but if they charge you tuition for internship credits, you're entitled to ask the university how it is earning its money. Universities do not earn the tuition they charge by requiring students to write papers about their academic internships. They earn their money by teaching. I would like more universities to do more in the way of placement, prepping, and checking in at mid-internship to see how student and employer are getting on. One way universities can earn that money is with extra programming, through career services, to help the students who pay for internship credits.

" Most people stop taking field trips after they leave grade school. Journalism is one field trip after another. We can knock on any door and ask questions. And if they don't let us in, we can go around to the back. **"**

—*John Maxwell Hamilton, journalist and journalism educator*

Graduate school

Many people who think about newspaper internships also think about grad school. In fact, a whole lot of people ask whether they should get a graduate degree in journalism. Here are some things to think about:

Ask yourself whether you're considering a master's degree because you want one or because you need one. If you have always wanted to get an advanced degree, you are acting on personal reasons quite distinct from career considerations. That's fine. If a master's is very important to you, perhaps that's reason enough to go for it.

If you're looking into a master's degree, decide whether you need to concentrate on theory or practice. Graduate programs tend to skew one way or the other. If you are looking to report and write better, to become a better visual journalist, or to grow in your news judgment and newsroom sophistication, find a grad school that focuses on the practical. If it is less important to you to gain practical skills, but you still want to get a master's degree, look at programs that focus on research and theory. Be skeptical of schools that claim they do both equally well. These are separate academic philosophies and they do not share power well. One generally dominates. Look at course descriptions. Usually, the decision to be one type of school or the other will be reflected in the course offering and in the school's culture.

Consider whether your additional studies need to be in journalism or something else. If you're a practicing journalist, what are you expecting to learn in a classroom that you haven't already learned in a newsroom? You may be able to benefit from a course in narrative or investigative journalism, but do you need to buy the whole program? Would a degree in law, politics, management, economics, criminology, or another specialty help you more? A great many editors will be more impressed if you add training and a credential in a supplemental area, rather than deepen your journalism. Some journalists, finding that the level of sophistication or feedback in their newsrooms is lacking, go to grad school to get what they need. Could they find it with a job change?

“I have never let my schooling interfere with my education.**”**

—Mark Twain

Guest: Grad school: If not for you, then who?

By LANITA PACE-HINTON
Director of Multimedia Training Programs
Knight New Media Center at University of California Berkeley Graduate
School of Journalism

Like many recruiters and hiring editors in the business, I was some-what dubious about the benefit of graduate journalism education. I believed that the best training one could get was through the real-life experience of the newsroom. However, after five years of working on staff at a graduate journalism school, observing the teaching and work-ing with students over the course of their studies, I have a different per-spective and greater appreciation for post-graduate journalism train-ing. While it is not a necessary stop for every would-be journalist en route to a professional career, it is a great staging ground for building skills and acquiring knowledge of the best practices and standards in the industry.

It seems to me that graduate journalism school is most advanta-geous to novices who decide late in their undergraduate college experi-ence that they want to become journalists. It is certainly beneficial to those working in other professions who want to parlay their curiosity about the world, their affinity for inquiry, and zeal for writing into a career in the press. And it can enhance the trajectories of those who have just a few years in the business and want to develop their craft away from the demands of daily deadlines.

Lanita Pace-Hinton has been the associate director of the Western Knight Center for Specialized Jour-nalism, managing WKC seminars held at the UC Berkeley. She began her journalism career as a fea-ture writer with Gannett News Service in Arlington, Virginia, and has written for the Detroit News and The Washington Post. Pace-Hinton joined The Press-Enterprise, in Riverside, California, as a reporter, and went on to serve as the assistant to the managing edi-tor responsible for editorial recruitment, coordinating the paper's internship programs and community outreach. She later taught jour-nalism and was the advisor to the student newspaper at Mount San Antonio College in Walnut, California.

Gaining entrée into the business necessitates not only classroom training, but also practical experience working for a college newspaper and, increasingly, multiple internships in professional newsrooms. For rising college seniors and recent graduates who have limited campus newspaper and internship experience, and those making career switches, graduate schools provide the opportunity to develop the essential experiences that will allow them to cast themselves as competitive candidates for newsroom jobs and perform well in the entry-level positions they will be hired into.

Young journalists who have spent two or three years working in small markets, weeklies, and alternative media can also benefit from the occasion graduate schools provide to rapidly expand their repertoire of reporting and writing skills away from the fast-paced workings of the newsroom. In addition to strengthening and advancing their fundamental reporting and writing abilities, graduate schools offer instruction in covering specialized topics such as business, the environment, and health, as well as courses in column writing, essay, long-form magazine pieces, multimedia storytelling, computerized data-based reporting, and advanced Internet research methods.

Many graduate journalism programs have international reporting components. These programs give journalists a chance to develop foreign reporting experiences that otherwise would not come until much later in their careers. Integral to these overseas reporting programs is the study of the social, historical, political, and economic makeup of the destination country as well as the past and current relationship between it and the United States.

Most graduate programs require that students write for publication, covering a standard beat for a local newspaper or for a news service. In addition, many programs guide students in producing and assist in placing special reporting projects in major metropolitan newspapers and national magazines. These experiences lead not only to an exceptional portfolio of writing samples, but they also provide the context for developing story conception and pitching skills, finding stories that fit editorial niches, recognizing common threads that transverse events, and knitting them together to show the larger themes and broader interest of local stories.

Just as vital as the training and experience are the contacts newcomers to the industry are able to establish with peers, mentors, and industry leaders. Journalism schools, graduate ones in particular, are nexuses for people within the industry—recruiters, editors, publishers, celebrity writers, etc., and are prime venues for networking. In a short span of time, diligent and astute students can rapidly build a substantial network of contacts that will be useful in their long-term professional development and career movement.

All that being said, when it comes to getting a job, it still boils down to the amount of real-life reporting and writing experience obtained by the end of the program. Contrary to a common misperception held by many prospective and current graduate school students, a master's degree in journalism, or any other subject matter, will not automatically vault graduates into the upper echelon of news companies or into the choice reporting positions at other companies. Only a select few, who possess the right combination of well-developed skills, experience, ambition, and savvy that fits the hiring criteria of the moment of top-tier news organizations, will be hired directly from school into these "destination" newsrooms. Most master's-level graduates begin their careers at small- to mid-size news organizations and work their way up the ranks of the newsroom and the industry. As these young journalists prove themselves in their entry-level posts, they can count on the array of skills and experiences gained in graduate school to help them accelerate through the freshman stages. ✹

Grad school myths—and truths

As you consider graduate schools, beware of some myths:

A master's degree means a bigger paycheck.
Some journalism schools perpetuate this myth. It's no wonder, as much as it costs to get a graduate degree. Some schools back up this assertion with comparisons on the starting salaries of people with undergrad and graduate degrees. The story starts to fall apart when, like good reporters, we ask questions. Do higher salaries for people with master's degrees have anything to do with the fact that master's students generally have more life experience and more journalistic experience than undergrads? Do the higher salaries have anything to do with the fact that grad students are looking at larger markets than undergrads? Grad schools annually graduate some people who came in with several years of professional experience on their résumés. It is misleading for the schools to imply that the higher salaries that these grads command are attributable solely to their degrees. The grad vs.

undergrad salary scorecard can be an apples vs. oranges comparison. Newspaper salary schedules are based on the level of experience. You won't find many newspaper job postings that ask for master's degrees. Newspapers believe that one becomes a journalist by doing journalism, not by studying about it. I know of no newspaper that has a higher salary scale based on level of education. The teaching profession pays more for degrees, but newspapers do not. If you are expecting to have grad school paid for by the higher salary you will command for having gone, you may be disappointed. There are many good reasons to earn a master's in journalism, but let's be realistic about the return on your investment.

If I don't get a master's now, it will be hard to get one later.
While work and life can get in the way of school, consider this: A lot of newspapers offer tuition reimbursement. That means that if you go to school part-time while working, the newspaper will reimburse you for some of your tuition. Check this out, though: most newspaper tuition-reimbursement programs offer far less than enough to cover full tuition, even for part-time programs. Several newspaper recruiters advise people to work for a few years before they go to grad school, so that they can get more out of the program. Journalism schools that have joint bachelor's and master's programs make it easy to earn one by staying in school, but may deprive the students of the benefits that experience can give a graduate student. Working journalists who return to school under an employer-financed tuition reimbursement program will do well to think about the timing. Reimbursements often carry a calendar-year cap. A person who starts in the fall, works through the

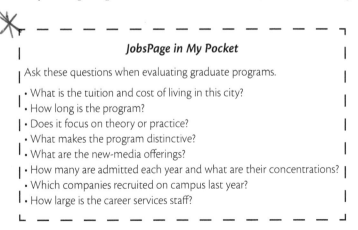

JobsPage in My Pocket

Ask these questions when evaluating graduate programs.

• What is the tuition and cost of living in this city?
• How long is the program?
• Does it focus on theory or practice?
• What makes the program distinctive?
• What are the new-media offerings?
• How many are admitted each year and what are their concentrations?
• Which companies recruited on campus last year?
• How large is the career services staff?

following year and finishes up the next spring can apply for reimbursement in three calendar years. A person who starts in January and who goes to school for the same number of months will be able to draw money in just two years.

A master's in journalism opens a lot of doors.

Part of this myth comes from good PR work on the part of journalism schools, which keep track of their alumni and trumpet the success stories, as they should. If you hear that a certain graduate program is supplying a lot of the talent to certain newspapers, flip the equation around. Ask what percentage of a given program's graduates is working at that newspaper. It will be small. You can do some good networking in some programs, but check it out.

A master's degree will command respect in the newsroom.

Journalists gain credibility from what they do inside of the newsroom, not so much for what they've done on the outside. If, however, grad school helps hone your skills, your news judgment and your leadership skills, your work will get the respect you're looking for. But it comes from what you learned and how well you apply it, not simply because of the credential. As a group, newspaper journalists are somewhere between being professionals, where academic credentials mean a lot, or craftspeople, who learn by working.

A master's degree will get you hired

One measure of success is how quickly graduates land jobs in journalism. Ask the admissions people to break the numbers down. If someone tells you that ninety percent of the program's graduates were placed ninety days after graduation, start asking: How many were in jobs and how many were in internships? How many of those positions were in journalism?

There are myths and there are benefits. These are some of the undeniable benefits you can get in journalism grad schools.

Networking

Some people go to graduate school as much for the connections as they do for the curriculum. Newspaper editors visit most of these programs to teach or recruit, and the graduate program can be one way to kick a career into a higher orbit. The power of some alumni networks—and the good reputation of people from those programs—is undeniable. The best J-schools can put you on recruiting main street where recruiters are concerned. They will come to your university to interview you for internships or jobs.

Teaching

Some journalists want to teach at the college level, and find that a master's degree helps qualify them for the position. However, not all universities require a master's. If part-time teaching is all you want and the local university will take you on as an adjunct without a master's, perhaps you don't need the additional degree.

Getting feedback

Some graduate students have said that they went back to school because they felt their journalism careers were plateauing and their editors were either unwilling or unable to give them the coaching they needed to rise. So, they traded the newsroom for the classroom and paychecks for tuition bills, just to get feedback.

Rising to a new level

Some folks, stymied at their present papers or range of papers, go after degree prestige to advance their careers. Sometimes it works, sometimes it doesn't. In all cases, it may have more to do with the individual than with the degree.

Find the situation that fits you

All this said, graduate school can be just the thing for igniting a career in journalism. Here are some additional thoughts, based on where you are in your career. Find the paragraph that best describes your situation:

Undergraduate journalism degree, but no experience: If you have taken a full load of journalism courses but did not get any experience beyond the student paper, it could be tough getting started in a good journalism job. In this case, people who go to graduate journalism school may not benefit from additional classroom work as much as from the connections and the additional semesters in which they can get professional internships.

Working journalist with a non-J undergraduate degree: If you are already doing journalism but want to feel the confidence that formal journalistic training can give you, J-school may provide it. Depending on your experience and proficiency, you might not need the basic training in reporting and writing. Try to get to the more advanced skills courses. Perhaps the university will count your work experience as evidence you have mastered prerequisite skills.

College graduate looking to transition into journalism: If you have an undergraduate degree outside of journalism and little to no recent journalism experience but want to break into the field, grad school is for you. But be very sure this is what you want before you invest the money and another year or two of your life in college. How do you find out? Spend several days visiting a newsroom and shadowing journalists. Freelance something. Choose a program that is oriented on the training and practice of journalism, not a communications research school.

Studying can help you find ways to do journalism better, but you will never be a journalist until you are reporting, writing, editing, photographing, designing, illustrating, and exercising your news judgment.

3

The Application

Even in the digital age, it still takes a lot of paper to land a good internship. An internship may be the first and last position you ever get strictly on the basis of what you can send through the mail. Many interns are hired sight unseen just because they present so well on paper. Think of internship applications as college applications without the transcripts—or the fees.

Internship applications typically have four or five parts:

- résumé
- cover letter
- clips
- references
- an essay, perhaps

Design your application so that the parts work together. They should complement each other. Go for reinforcement rather than redundancy. Try to use an array to your advantage. That's harder than it sounds because every editor is different. This one will start with the résumé and that one will start with the clips. Another will begin with the essay or will recognize a familiar name among your references. Because you won't know who is reading your material—or how they are reading it—you'll have to be able to capture an editor's attention with every part—no matter where the editor decides to start.

If an editor starts with clips that are bland, why should she read the letter? Why read the résumé if the cover is a wet-blanket letter? You can order your material any way you like—typically, cover letter, résumé, references, clips, essay—but editors will reshuffle your package to suit their routines. Candidates sometimes ask whether I read their internship applications. I look at each one. But I do not need to plough through every page of every application to make good decisions. Sometimes, a single page will tell me that this candidate is not as promising as the others. So, make every part a strong entry point that encourages editors to look at the other parts, too. A résumé can refer to tasty stories in the clip package. So can a cover letter. An essay can hint that the résumé contains some surprises. Get the editor's attention—and hold it. The more time we spend with the bait, the more likely we are to bite.

Let's consider how the parts can mesh, and then look at them individually.

The résumé is the who, what, where, and when of your career. Your cover letter should be the why. The clips show how you do the work.

Don't use your cover letter to tell what's already on your résumé. That's being redundant. Use the cover letter to explain how the résumé came to be that way, or to go between the lines and show what you learned about journalism and yourself in some of those experiences.

The essay, if requested, goes in another direction. In it, you show your writing in a more natural state, you talk about your ideas and you show the connection between your personal and professional sides. Tell why you are passionate about journalism (or at least curious about it) and what your goals are. These angles are out of place on a résumé and they may be too complicated to explain in a cover letter. Now, you have distinct purposes for résumé, cover letter, and essay.

Résumés

When it comes to selling yourself on paper, you will find newspaper editors to be tough audiences. And it's no wonder. Most are pretty familiar with serving up information on paper. They don't give bonus points if you spell everything correctly or if you have good punctuation or grammar. Those should be givens. A single error can consign your résumé to the circular file. Edit your work, proofread it, and double-check everything. Twice. Have someone else go over it. Make sure the editor is *not* the first person to see the finished product.

Understand the purpose of a résumé. It is not meant to get you a job. It is meant to tell prospective employers enough about you so that they'll be intrigued, see a place for you in their program, look at your work and consider you. The résumé is preliminary. It is Square One.

In a business of word economists, one-page résumés have been the tradition for decades. This is changing, though not with all editors. Even editors with twenty years and several papers behind them limit their own résumés to one page and expect that internship candidates, new to the business, can, too. You're certainly free to exceed a page, but the penalty is that some editors will brush the whole application aside. No one will reject a one-page résumé for its length.

Content

What comes after name, address, phone number and e-mail?
A line stating your career objective can help, but only if it matches the opening. An objective that is incompatible with the opening eliminates you in a New York minute. I am still surprised at how many people apply to my newspaper saying they want to work in broadcast. They make my job easy.

In most cases, your objective will be obvious from the fact that you're applying. The best time to use an objective line is if the job you're applying for is different from your education and experience. Then, you'll need to say something like, "To apply my training as a sociologist to journalism."

In most cases, you'll lead off with a section about your education or experience. But which one? Lead off with the one that seems to you to be more impressive. If you have experience at a daily newspaper, you will almost always want to put the experience section at the top of your résumé. If all your work has been outside journalism, but you have a degree in it, lead with the degree and highlights of your coursework to beef it up. If you're completing a non-journalism degree and have two internships at newspapers, list the internships first. The categories' chronological order is less important than relevance. However, follow chronological order *within* categories, most recent to oldest.

The Edge ————————————————————————————
Before you e-mail your résumé to an editor, e-mail a copy to yourself. Check it for glitches and bad formatting.

Go beyond simple job titles

Describe your jobs. Don't just say you were a reporter. Say you were a reporter who covered a school district, two police departments and the local court and that you wrote a Sunday column. Animate your résumé by mentioning your more complicated, difficult, or humorous accomplishments. Details distinguish your résumé from others, tell the newspaper something about your interests and abilities and you can boost your chances. Give your résumé some personality.

Do I include non-journalism jobs?

If you have a short employment history, you certainly may include jobs that are not journalism-related. These demonstrate that you know how to toil for a living, work for others, show up on time, and generally act responsibly. Stress skills that are most similar to newspapering: writing, handling information, working with the public, juggling tasks.

What else should I include?

Second languages if you are skilled enough to interview in them, awards, scholarships, and extracurricular activities are all good. Highlight those that demonstrate leadership, resourcefulness, tenacity, or responsibility. One student impressed me because she juggled full-time care-giving with a full load of classes.

Omit personal information …

Your résumé should not include the personal information such as age or date of birth, marital status, or whether you smoke. Employers are not supposed to ask about those things, so you look naïve if you just come right out and tell.

… But include interesting side notes

My curiosity is piqued when someone's résumé carries a list of places visited or lived in. Generally, the more relevant an item is to the job, the safer it is to use. Being accomplished at a musical instrument, for example, implies precision, discipline, and practice. I thought people who listed "coffee" under hobbies or "Costco" under memberships were showing that they had a sense of humor, but this might leave some recruiters cold. Every editor is different.

Design

While the content of your résumé is No. 1, its appearance says something about you, too.

A clear résumé has a structure. It is designed on a grid.

At the top of every résumé there is a section with your name and contact information. That should be a mailing address, one or more phone numbers and an e-mail address. Don't signify which is the e-mail address by saying "E-mail." Nothing else looks like an e-mail address. Signify which is your home phone and which is your cell. Never put a work phone number on a job application and don't use company stationery for your application.

Going across the grid, there should be two or three columns: left margin, right margin and one you set as an indent. Down these columns, line up dates, the names of universities or companies and perhaps a column for job titles. At intervals down the page are horizontal lines, like headlines. These may be major headings, such as "education," "experience," or "additional skills," or sub-headlines, such as the names of universities or employers.

A good résumé is chronological, of course. Education may be at the top, if you don't have much experience yet, or at the bottom, if you have some jobs to talk about. While education may span more years than jobs for internship candidates, and while it may be ongoing, it is fine to put education at the bottom, even if that looks to be out of chronological order. It will be fine, as long as you keep it chronological within headings.

Once you have the hang of organizing information on a grid, you can start to experiment for a unique look. On my résumé, I put education in a column down the right side. I've seen some attractive résumés where the name and contact information runs up the left side. But in all these cases, we stick to a grid that keeps things organized.

It's all right to be bold, but be careful about being too flashy. I have seen cartoon résumés, résumés with little basketballs on them and ré-

The Edge ————————————————————————————
If you want your résumé paper to stand out in a classy way, choose stock that is textured or that has a little extra weight, but that is close to white. Bright colors look cheesy. Some colored papers, though muted, are so dark they do not photocopy well. Avoid paper with little specks that could look like accent marks or punctuation that could confuse a scanner—or an editor.

sumés made to look like front pages. Tricked-up résumés suggest you lack sophistication or experience. Circus résumés *will* make you stand out—outside the pool of finalists.

Stick with standard-size paper, as these applications are headed for file folders. Be restrained with type styles. We do not need to see all the fonts you have on your computer.

If you have the ambition and the skill to get more involved in résumé design, go to a good bookstore, look for a volume on résumés. Page through it until you see something that seems to reflect the image you're trying to send and that looks professional. Try that style.

Guest: Time management in the job search

By WALTER T. MIDDLEBROOK
Director of Recruiting and Community Relations
The Detroit News

Sixty seconds. S-I-X-T-Y seconds. That's all you get.

Whether it's in the reading of your cover letter, the browsing of your résumé, or after you've sat down for that all-important job interview. All you get, Mr. or Ms. Job Candidate, is sixty seconds.

Within that sixty seconds, most job interviewers, I suspect, make a decision on whether it's worth their time to pursue you as a job candidate for any potential opening at their respective organizations.

Sixty seconds. That's right. And I may be a little generous here. Think I'm pulling your leg? Think about it. And sixty seconds is really a lot longer than you think.

Take a break right now. Spend the next sixty seconds doing absolutely nothing. You can stare at this sentence. You can stare at your watch. But other than that relax and do nothing else.

Hold on . . . Keep holding on.

Did you think that minute would ever end? Well that eternity is just long enough for an employer to assess your ability to sell yourself. And the question each job candidate needs to answer: Are you using your sixty seconds wisely?

If you sit down for an interview and it takes forever to tell the employer what job you are seeking and why you think you're qualified to fill that position, you've wasted your sixty seconds.

If your résumé starts off listing your educational achievements while you're really seeking full-time employment as a copy editor or news producer, you've wasted your sixty seconds.

If your cover letter is a rehash of your résumé instead of telling a great story about how you approach your work or how you've impressed your former employers, you've wasted your sixty seconds.

It is these subtle time-consuming actions that can hurt a job candidate's hiring quotient. You've got sixty seconds. Use them wisely.

A cover letter is one of the best opportunities to show your writing skills. But if it's the "I am . . . , I did . . . , I was . . . " formatted letter, you've wasted your sixty seconds. And there is nothing in your packet that's going to make any potential employer visualize the creativity that you contend is hidden in your soul once they've reached that conclusion.

Look at that clip file or the tape you've been passing out. If your best two or three stories are not leading the pack, you have wasted your sixty seconds.

A young man's packet arrived on my desk some time ago. After the first eight horribly written stories, I came across a jewel in his packet.

"Do you think an editor has the time to read through all this to find this story?" I asked. By the time most editors would have gotten through the first four stories, they would have determined that this young man could not write. These editors might never have seen that ninth story, I suggested.

His response: "I put them in chronological order."

If you want someone to get interested in you, you'd better use your sixty seconds to hit that employer with your best shot. Don't worry about chronology, unless you're trying to show the progression of a series of stories. Show your work—best to worse.

Take your résumé: Why hide your contact information? Why hide what kind of work you can do or that you want to do? Why hide your

Walter T. Middlebrook, director of recruiting and community relations at The Detroit News, has been associate editor for recruitment at Newsday, where he was responsible for all newsroom recruiting and the paper's internship programs. He also oversaw the Tribune Co.'s METpro/Editing program.

qualifications? And if you're thinking about a career/job change, tell the employer where you see yourself going and how it fits in that company's picture. And do it in that first sixty seconds.

Hiding your address, phone numbers, and e-mail address (if you included it at all), is not helping your cause. Permanent addresses are a MUST. If you're in the early stages of your career, you're going to move. If an employer has to search to find you, your sixty seconds have been wasted.

The simple rule: Don't make a potential employer have to work to find out about you. Give up that information right away. That gives you more time to sell yourself.

Job candidates must look upon their résumé, their cover letter, their interview just as they look at the lead of that Page One news story that's being prepared for tomorrow's publication or tonight's newscasts.

Get to the facts, and do it in that first sixty seconds. Tick, tick, tick . . . ✹

Cover letters

I love it when things begin to drop in autumn. Each one unique, they shout for attention as they flutter to me, hundreds upon hundreds of them, swirling into big piles.

We're not talking leaves here. This is the fall harvest of internship applications. But this is about as far as the similarities go. I rake and bag the leaves. I read the applications, and I don't let anyone near them with yard tools.

Interns have a tougher time than anyone else with cover letters because they arrive in such a flurry and because all have such similar backgrounds. Even mid-size newspapers get hundreds of applications for a handful of spots. But there's hope—and help.

The challenge is to stand out from the crowd. With résumés looking so similar by necessity, this raises the ante on the cover letter. Most cover letters from internship candidates are unremarkable. Use yours to find an advantage.

Here are some opening leads culled or paraphrased from internship applications.

If your letter starts like those in these first two groups, you likely are in the unchosen majority. Find a new style . . . maybe something from the later groups.

Experiment with gentle combinations, say, an opening line with a twist to get an editor's attention, and then an autobiographical body. Write in a style that reflects your own experience and interests. Don't strain. Notice that some of the better leads are really combinations.

Bland

Many internship candidates, writing cover letters for perhaps the first time in their lives, go for the safe—and bland. They state facts obvious from the résumé or the return address or the signature at the bottom of the letter. Be more imaginative than that. Make every word count.

I am applying for a summer photo internship with the *Daily Tidings* because I know I can do the job well.

I currently am a senior majoring in journalism and minoring in psychology at Party Tech. In addition, I . . .

My name is John Doe, and I am a sophomore in the process of completing a bachelor's degree in journalism at the University of Gigantic Proportions.

I am writing you concerning a possible internship. I feel that I will be an asset to you and your staff for many reasons.

I am Jane Doe, a junior at Anonymous State University, applying for your summer internship.

I recently became aware of your internship program and am interested in exploring opportunities with your newspaper.

I understand that you are looking for a feature writing intern for the summer.

My name is John Doe. I would very much like to be considered for . . .

My name is Jane Doe and I am a sophomore at State University in What's-its-town, New York. . . .

I am a junior at Studious U., majoring in journalism and planning a career as a newspaper reporter. . . .

Wordy

A close cousin of the bland letters, these spend a great deal of time in throat-clearing. Get to the point quickly—just as editors want reporters to.

I am currently looking for a summer internship in the print journalism industry and would like to be considered for such a position at your newspaper. I am a junior in college pursuing a concentration in print journalism and would very much appreciate a chance to apply what I have learned at a first-rate newspaper, such as yours.

It has come to my attention through an advertisement at Big State University that intern positions in feature writing are available at your newspaper.

I am writing to express my interest in an internship at the *Afternoon Delight* over the coming summer.

I would like to use this letter as an opportunity to introduce myself as a qualified candidate for the summer internship program at the *Daily Ordeal*.

Tell a story:

Journalists tell stories. Show the editor that you can by doing it. If you take this approach, be sure to slip your point in early.

Each day, Barb Shook carried an armful of shirts into the dry cleaners, and picked up a few clean ones, neatly pressed and bagged in plastic. Working the counter to pay for my journalism studies, I was intrigued by the woman with all the shirts. Finally, I just had to ask . . .

It's surprising how quickly you can wear out a pair of shoes on the streets of Chicago. . . .

Reading my notes by flashlight and typing on a laptop as someone I had just met drove me through a driving rainstorm, I knew I was in the right business.

When Jim Johnson appeared to chase his family out of the house and then set fire to it, the neighbors thought he was acting crazy again. It turns out, he was a hero.

My parents told me that, if I was going to go out of state to go to school, then I'd have to get there on my own. In a borrowed car that became my living quarters for the next four days, I did.

The Edge ────────────────────────────────────

Don't overdo the story. Some recruiters have said that this is a turnoff for them. A former recruiter for *The Washington Post* said she had read way too many letters describing heroic journalists filing stories under impossibly perilous conditions. She just wanted them to tell her what they wanted. Because you can't know the preferences of every editor, be brief, be good, don't go overboard.

Experienced:
Many internship candidates have only slight experience. If you have loads of experience compared to what you think your competition has, work it.

In two summer internships, I have written more than one hundred stories on everything from a murder-suicide to a neighborhood bicycle parade.

As an editor of my campus newspaper, I hold the record for . . . (let's hope this is something journalistic.)

Few reporters my age can say that they've met the president and been thrown out of the local police station for asking too many questions. . . .

I have endured horseflies, poison ivy, angry dogs, and downpours to get a good quote or a telling detail for a story. . . .

I absolutely loved working at the *Small Town Crier*. . . .

After a city desk internship at the *Suburban Scribe* and two terms editing my school paper, I am ready to go to work for the . . .

The direct approach:
If you're proud of who you are and are a what-you-see-is-what-you-get person, try the fresh and straightforward approach. What would you tell the editors, face to face, games aside, about why they should hire you? Be crisp. Be concise.

Please accept my application for a photo internship at the *No-Nonsense News*. I believe that my experience at school and in a prior internship, as well as my knowledge of the area, make me a strong candidate for your newspaper.

Hire me for a sports internship because I work tirelessly, find stories everywhere, and write them well.

My passion is to tell stories. . . .

Twist:
Wake up the editor with a twist or a tease. Play contradiction, misdirection, or irony to your advantage. Remember that one of the key things editors want to find in a good cover letter is evidence that you can write.

Like most student journalists, I expected to start at the bottom with dog shows, planning commission meetings and ribbon-cutting ceremonies. That's not what I got, though, when I showed up for the first day of work last summer . . .

Sometimes, the stories I tell amaze me. . . .

It's been said that you're only as good as your last story. Let me tell you what it was. . . . (this carries an obvious hook to your clip package.)

One of several dozen routine announcements from the campus public information office contained the germ of a story that led to a resignation.

I have to admit, I wasn't excited the first time I was asked to cover the city council.

I never wanted to be a journalist. Now, I can't help it.

Confident:

A narrow line to walk, be bold without being brash, assured without being arrogant. Only you know whether such an approach is natural to you. The last two examples here would turn me off, but that's me.

I am exactly the right person for your sports-writing internship.

Are you looking for a highly motivated, team-centered, up-and-coming reporter who is hard working and creative? I am that person.

There are few guarantees in life. I am one. Hire me, and you will not be disappointed.

You've been looking for someone who will bring creativity, energy, and initiative to your newsroom. I am that person.

Congratulations! You have just found the perfect intern.

The person you have been looking for has applied.

Autobiographical and interesting:

Can you tell a story about yourself that explains why you are an excellent prospect? These letters key on character traits that make for good journalists.

My family always said I loved to tell stories.

Perhaps it's my sense of order that led me to newspaper design.

Since the age of seven, I have known that this was the right business for me.

Maybe it was destiny, because it sure wasn't heredity.

It's only natural, I suppose, that the girl who spent so many hours in the library reading stories would one day be writing them.

All the hours I spent in journalism class didn't teach me as much about reporting as the hours I spent driving a hack.

As a senior in high school, I swore I'd never leave my home and family. I did, though, kicking and screaming, and it was the best thing I ever did.

Four years ago, being a reporter was the furthest thing from my mind. Now, I can't think of anything else.

I never really felt at home at college—until I walked into the student newspaper.

Math was never my strong suit.

As the math whiz in my high school, I was the last person anyone ever expected would want to write for a living. Now I can't imagine things any other way.

I've been preparing for this internship ever since I became a journalist—in the second grade.

Clips

Clips are critical. They are the tickets for admission to virtually any job in the newspaper business. No clips? No chance.

So what are clips? And what are not clips?

Clips are samples of your published work. They may be photocopies, they may be Web printouts, but they must have been published. Ideally, they should have been published by a newspaper or magazine. Alternatively, they may have been published by a Web site or newsletter. Work published in student publications is OK, but student clips are not regarded as highly as work published in professional publications.

Class assignments, no matter how journalistically sound, are not clips. They have not been published and cannot be literally or figuratively clipped. If you submit unpublished work as clips, you will seem naïve. The fact that someone has no real clips while so many other candidates do eliminates them immediately.

So, get clips.

The Edge

❝ Whether you're preparing for a job interview or to send out clips, always do your reporting first. Your research will help you come up with questions for the interview or formulate a cover letter for your packet.❞

—*Randy Hagihara, Los Angeles Times*

Campus publications

The easiest way for students to get clips is at campus publications. Most large universities have more than one, so if the first won't let you in or is not right for you, keep looking. You need to get clips.

People often tell me that they are in a Catch-22. "No one will hire me without experience, but if no one hires me, how do I get it?"

I try to be sympathetic, but I don't buy it.

If they are writing to me, they are sending this question to a major metro newspaper. That is not the place to start.

Obviously, some people are getting their starts somewhere, or all the newsrooms in the country would be empty.

Start at the college newspaper. That is, for many people, the first step. It is unrealistic to complain that the *New York Times* won't hire you when you have never worked for the campus paper, the small-town weekly, or your local daily. That's how most of those people at the *New York Times* started. You need to do that, too.

Most student pubs need more help, although a few take only up-perclassmen or are very selective about whom they'll let in the door. Fortunately, these cases usually occur only at large campuses, where you can find other, more open publications.

If the main student newspaper won't take you, try the alternative. If there isn't one, look for a magazine. Don't forget the yearbook. Wherever you see a publication, there is a potential to work for clips.

You won't get rich working for campus publications, but you will learn a lot about your interests and abilities, and these clips are the admission tickets you need to get into the newspaper business. Even internships require prior clips.

Local newspapers

There are mainstream and alternative newspapers near every college campus. A lot of them need news about the college and welcome students' work, provided it's well reported, well written, and on time. For someone who's just starting out, no publication is too small. Pick up the newspapers and tabloids you find around campus and find the editors' names inside. Call them and set up an appointment to talk with them about stringing opportunities. Study several issues. Walk into the interview with knowledge of what the newspaper or magazine publishes, and ideas for articles. You want to be able to walk away from the interview with an assignment. It probably will have to be a story you pitch, as they may be reluctant to give a story from their idea list to an untested writer.

Out-of-town newspapers

The Big U (and almost every little one, too) attracts people from all kinds of places. Their hometown newspapers want stories about Local Boy as Big Man on Campus. If an out-of-town student is big on a sports team or in some other way, a profile of her might be of interest to the paper back home and, especially if it's a smaller paper, they'd love to have you write something for them. Don't forget pictures. If you can't take pictures, find someone who does—maybe one of the photographers whose name you see in the student newspaper. Use the *Editor & Publisher Year Book* to look up the addresses, phone numbers, and contacts of out-of-town newspapers. If you're attending a school away from home, start by looking for stories of interest to your hometown paper. You can drop in on them while you're home for the holidays.

One of my journalism students said that he wanted to be a sports writer, but was worried because he had no clips. Our class was meeting about ten miles from where the Detroit Pistons play their home basketball games. I told him to contact mid-size newspapers on the outskirts of cities with National Basketball Association teams. He was to ask if they would like to have him do something special for them, something that went beyond what they and all their suburban competitors could get from wire services. We figured that the big papers would send their own writers, but that at some level we would find papers that wanted their own stories, but could not afford to send someone.

The very next week, he came to class, flush with the story of how he had watched the game from the press box on a pass arranged by one of these papers, which had asked him to do a story. He had been courtside, he had been on TV, he had met other sports writers. He had a clip.

The Edge ───
Take extra copies of you résumé and clips to a job interview. You don't want to be stuck if the newspaper has not distributed them.

"Who did you write for?" I asked.
"The *Boulder Daily Camera*."
"That's a good paper. How did you choose it?"
"I just looked up the next team on the schedule. It was Denver."
Fair enough.

Specialty publications

Many universities are big on research and have experts in their field. Every field has a magazine or Web site these days, and you can write for them. Find out what your school is known for, and find out what kind of work is going on. Very often, departments publish small bulletins about who's studying this or researching that. Once you've identified a new research wrinkle, try to find a market for an article about it. The place to look is *Writer's Market*. Like *E&P*, it is updated every year and is probably sitting on a shelf at the reference desk. Also like *E&P*, it contains names, numbers and even gives the magazines' editorial needs. Send the magazine a query in which you pitch an article about developments on your campus. The Internet has made it so much easier for us to freelance articles for distant places.

Nonprofits

Can't find anyone to pay you for your work? Work for free. Nonprofits often have newsletters—even magazines—that will publish your work, even though they won't give you money. Get over the money issue and work for the clips—at least initially. As soon as you can, parlay those clips into something that pays. In exchange for your free work, ask for some editing and direction.

Sell your homework

For many students, the obstacle to getting those first clips is not finding someone to write for, but finding the time. Here's where to find it: You're doing lots of writing for your classes. Make those writing assignments do double duty. If a professor assigns a journalistic piece on a subject, find a market for it before you begin writing. Check *Writer's Market* or *E&P*. Call the publication to determine its interest in an article. Then approach the prof. Many profs are proud to see their students' work published. Sometimes a simple change in the assignment—or just submitting it—will let you write for class and for clips at the same time. You might even be able to find a deal that lets you write for credit, clips, and cash. Once, for a class assignment I had to write a profile turned into a magazine article on a young fencer in the area who was nationally ranked.

Freelancing

More often than you might expect, people ask me how they can possibly get any experience if everyone tells them they do not have enough experience to get hired.

They just need to start smaller. Freelancing can be a great way to get clips when no one will hire you. It can also be a great way to get the clips you need to land an internship, especially if the collegiate press is closed off to you because your school doesn't have a paper, it won't hire you, or you are a late bloomer.

Almost all internships require at least six published clips for writing positions. Freelancing is an excellent way to get clips and it can be a good substitute for a first internship.

People freelance for newspapers for other reasons. Some like having just a little journalism in their lives, and cannot or would not take full-time newspaper jobs. Others do it for clips, hoping to parlay those into internships or jobs. And a few entrepreneurs are full-time freelancers, working for a stable of publications and preferring to remain self-employed.

A freelancer called our paper and asked for a freelance assignment. We didn't know the person, didn't have an assignment for her to try and didn't pursue the matter.

But the freelancer did.

She read our paper, figured out what we covered—and what we were missing—and went to a local city's meeting on her own. The meeting was a hot one, and we were not there. So, she called us the next day to pitch her story. She got into the paper and onto our stringer list.

She followed this system:

First, learn about the publication. Do that by reading it. If you don't

---

❝A good many young writers make the mistake of including a stamped, self-addressed envelope, big enough for the manuscript to come back in. This is too much of a temptation to the editor.**❞**

—*Ring Lardner*

know what the publication uses, what it has already published or its style, you cannot pitch effectively.

Second, as you read, try to determine where freelance material appears. Look for subtle difference in bylines. If someone is referred to as a correspondent or special writer, rather than the way most reporters are described, these likely are freelancers. Sometimes, a tagline at the end of an article will even tell you that a freelancer wrote the piece. This will tell you which departments have budgets for freelancers. It makes little sense to try to sell freelance pieces to editors who have no budget for it.

Once you have determined the sections for which you would like to write, based on your interests and the newspaper's receptivity to freelance pieces, you need to come up with a story idea. Newspapers rarely will give story ideas to untried freelancers. Editors want to know that you'll produce before they'll let you tie up one of their story ideas. But if you come with the idea, they may let you show what you can do with it. Do not write the article before talking with the editor. Some people like to write their articles without outside influence. This is the wrong approach. When you have a story idea, pitch it to an editor and land the assignment. Then find out more. How long does the editor want this to be? What is the deadline? Does he or she have any preference for the angle or direction of the piece? What about art? You want to come, as close as possible, to giving editors exactly what they want, especially on a first assignment. Failure to meet the editor's needs or standards can make any freelance piece your last one.

Pitch your story to the right editor. Make some calls, do some reporting and find out whom you should be talking to. As the recruiter at my newspaper, I get a lot of calls and e-mails from people wanting to freelance for us. When I redirected one caller to the proper editor, he then e-mailed me to ask the person's e-mail and phone number. When I told him he could find it on the newspaper's Web site, he e-mailed again to say that he couldn't and to ask me to give him the specific information. How will this person ever manage to write an article if he can't find an editor's phone number on a Web site? Be self-sufficient.

Increasingly, newspapers are asking people to sign freelance agreements. These explain the rights of the newspaper and the freelancer in this transaction. You cannot generally negotiate changes in the agreement. It's either sign it or forget it, so if you want to do this article or photo and future ones, you'll have to sign off. The agreement may stipulate that the article becomes the newspaper's property and that the newspaper can re-use it, say, on its Web site, or let it circulate on a wire service. While you might like to get paid as many times as your work gets used, keep in mind that greater circulation does have some non-monetary value to you and, as we are working for newspapers, we are creating goods that do not have much shelf life.

Magazines prefer story queries to come by mail, but you'll likely have better luck phoning newspaper editors. News is perishable and you can get a lot more done much more quickly on the phone.

After you have published one piece with the newspaper, look for more. You have done the difficult set-up work of breaking the ice and starting a relationship. You won't have to do that for the next story, The more repeat work you can do, the less time you'll have to spend making contacts and selling yourself, and the more time you'll have to do what you like.

People who want to make freelancing their full-time jobs find more security and steadier income by building a stable of clients with a few that pay regular and decent paychecks, and supplementing those clients with others upon whom they are less dependent.

Write for the Web

The Internet puts many publications within easy reach. A lot of them are on the prowl for content. This creates a lot of opportunities, though they may be low-paying. Editors will accept Web printouts as clips, but try to get them with the most established and respected online publi-

---

JobsPage in My Pocket

When you get the editor on the phone, ask these questions to ensure the best possible experience (for the editor) with your article or photos.

When do you want it?
How many words (or images) would you like?
Can I provide anything that might help us with a photo or graphic?
How would you like to receive the article or photos?
How should I handle cutlines?
Do you have a particular angle or structure in mind?
What section or audience should I be aiming for?
Do you have my e-mail and cell phone? I am always available.

cations you can, because editors place higher emphasis on reputation and quality with online publications than they do with print pubs.

Start your own

This is not for the timid. If you can't find an in with any publications, maybe it's time to start something new. Look for a niche—sports, music, culture—and fill it with your own publication. Experience tells us that new publications usually do not last long, but you'll learn a ton, work hard and have some fun. You'll also have, even more than clips, a good experience to use in landing that internship.

Presentation

Editors usually want to see six to ten clips. It is best to send no more than that, unless requested.

A good clip package will contain articles without mistakes, predominantly with single bylines, and a selection that shows you have different approaches. Let's examine each point:

- **Mistakes in clips:** I am sorry—really sorry—that one of your best clips has a great, big blob of a mistake in it. You shouldn't use it as

The Edge

The words "stringing" and "freelancing," which mean essentially the same thing, have interesting origins.

The term stringing comes from measuring the length of one's stories in the paper by holding a string alongside the column. One can keep track of the combined length of stories—or one long story spread over several columns—by knotting the string at the end of each column and then measuring the next. At the end of the pay period, one need only measure the length of the string to come up with the total number of inches published.

In medieval times, a "free-lance," was a knight without a castle who was free to fight for whoever would pay for his services. Free-lance writers are not on the payroll and work for whoever will pay them. Staff member may be allowed to "freelance" work outside their job descriptions at their own papers.

an example of your work. Of course you did not make the mistake yourself, but that won't help you much. Either you made the mistake, or you work for a publication that does. Lose it.

- **Single-byline clips:** The clearest sign that you did the work is if yours is the only name on the story. Everyone gets edited, of course, but multiple-bylined stories can obscure which parts of the reporting and writing are yours. You may add a note to such a clip, if it is one of your best, and mark the parts of the article that are yours, but don't send more than one or two. A story with multiple bylines can be a plus, as most dailies will swarm the big stories, and we want to know that yo can collaborate.
- **Variety:** Your clip package should show your range within the area where you're applying. If you are applying for a metro reporting job, show breaking news, news you broke (that is something different), a profile, a good feature story, and an explanatory piece, if you can. At least make sure you're showing different kinds of leads. Some editors will give a quick first glance at your leads. If they sound similar, that might imply that you have limited range.

How to mount clips

Use the KISS formula: Keep it Simple, Sweethearts. Photocopies are perfectly fine. So are printouts from the Web. Do not clean up your clips. While it may be tempting to repair the mistake that someone else made in your clip, never, ever do that. It's not honest.

Do not waste your time or money buying elaborate folders or portfolios, mounting your clips in plastic sleeves or mounting them in those cardboard folders with the scary prongy things.

One of the first things we do is shuck the peripherals. Think about it. The handiest way for us to photocopy applications or to put them in our manila-folder files is if the clips, résumé, cover letter, etc. arrive wearing nothing more than a paper clip.

With that in mind, you can understand the value of making your clips the standard, U.S. letter size.

What do you do if your clips are larger than that, as newspaper clips often are? Two things not to do:

- Don't shrink the type. Many editors, like me, are in the Bifocals Club. We cannot admire what we cannot read.

- Don't send them at their actual size, all flapping around as L-shaped or T-shaped cutouts that are harder to refold than highway maps.

Smart things you can do:

- Cut the story apart and paste it (double check that you have it in order) on letter-size paper. Photocopy those master sheets.
- Submit Web-page printouts of your writing.
- Best: Make letter-size printouts of whole pages where your clips appeared and follow it with Web printouts or the paste-ups. Ask someone at the newspaper to show you how to make printouts of pages. They often are in a Portable Document Format, called .pdf for short.

Copy-editing clips

Copy editors have it tougher than most. Few editors will take the time to wade through before and after versions of an article that someone edited. Here are three strategies copy editors can use to display their work:

- Send a sheet of just headlines. They should be clear, compelling, difficult to write and clear without the context of the articles.
- Send stories that have been published, but include a side note that tells how you improved the article. One student from the University of Missouri called these deconstructions.
- Best of all: Send an article you have edited that show your editing changes within the body of the original article. Then the editor can follow along with you. Word offers this in its "Track changes" option. Some mainframe editing programs do to in "notes mode" or story versions.

The Edge —————————————————————————————

A date and name of publication gives editors the context for your clips. Most internship seekers just write those on the page. You'll look neater if you put the date and publication on a backing sheet using the same font you used in your cover letter or résumé. Print it out, mount your clip on that and make the photocopy.

- Remember that editors will scrutinize a copy editor's résumé, cover letter, and other material more closely as actual work samples than they will scrutinize the work of people applying for other sorts of internships. Be letter-perfect.

Photography and videography

Photographers are in a whole different realm when it comes to clips. The digital revolution has helped photographers immensely. No longer should they be sending books of prints or sheets of transparencies. That was all very time-intensive and expensive. Now, work should be put on a CD with a program that makes it easy for photo directors to click through them. Put the work into a slide show using a program like Quick Show that is compatible with both Macs and PCs. Do not just plop a bunch of single images with meaningless names onto the CD. That will require editors to open and close each image in turn. That's tedious. Make your show flow from one to the next on a timer or with a simple click on a link.

Another exception for photographers: Your work does not need to have been published. Most directors of photography are happy to look at your unpublished work or a mix of published and unpublished.

Photographers need to submit more items than writers do. Start with twenty singles and a photo story with a clear middle, beginning, and end should do the trick. Photographers today should also know how to shoot and edit video, so a video clip you produced should be there. At minimum, send an audio slide show with your still photography. Variety is still key. Send sports, news, and features; breaking news, portraits, and studio work.

Spend a lot of time on your captions and have a good copy editor check them over. Directors of photographer are understandably skittish about photojournalists who don't get their facts right.

Art and design

The story here is much the same as it is for photographers: Use a digital medium and send more than the half-dozen clips that editors typically want to see from writers.

Designers and, more recently, artists have taken to the Web in some numbers to show and share their wares. Design and graphics directors now lead the newsroom in being comfortable with portfolios that are Web-based.

References

Your internship application may be one of the first times you are asked to give professional references. Professional references are distinct from personal or character references. A professional reference can comment on your abilities and performance in relation to work.

Smart people begin to cultivate references long before they need them. Generally, employers ask for at least three and will check with at least two of those—and perhaps some you don't list.

Where can you find good professional references for a first internship? They generally come from three areas. One, of course, is from any kind of professional work you did in journalism. It likely won't be a full-blown job, but it could be freelancing for a local newspaper, being selected as finalist for a scholarship or doing some kind of work at a paper.

When the *Free Press* covers local elections, we hire as many as twenty students to work with us on election night. I bring in journalism students. I tell the students that working the election can be an early résumé builder and could even lead to a limited reference. I pay attention to how they do and ask other people at the paper how they did. If someone fails to show or slacks off, I do not ask them back. If they hustle and excel, I try to invite them back and can give a little reference on them. Professional references—from real editors at real newspapers—are your best ones.

Next best are professors, advisors, placement directors and other professionals in the university community who can say good things about your work in class or around campus. They might be asked about your ability to meet deadlines, the quality of your work, your work ethic, and the leadership you demonstrate.

Third best are employers who can comment on your work habits at non-journalism jobs.

Do not list editors at your campus paper. Many of us will not call one student to ask about another. There is a good chance that the student you list as a reference might be a competitor for the internship. For all we know, it is a boyfriend or girlfriend. Or an ex. Cultivate professors or advisors instead.

If your résumé is getting too crowded for one page, use a second sheet just for references. Most editors will still see this as a one-page résumé.

Don't say "References available upon request." Just list them.

Essays

Like many universities, some newspapers ask internship applicants to submit personal essays. For a lot of people, this is the most stressful part of the written application. They wonder why the newspaper is asking for such detail. They want to know what is left to say after the cover letter and résumé.

This is why newspapers ask for essays, and some strategies for writing your own.

Here are three reasons newspapers require essays:

- To find out how interested you really are. We get a lot of applications. They are dropped off, e-mailed in, sent by overnight mail, and delivered in face-to-face interviews at the newspaper and on campuses in other states. We get To-Whom-it-May-Concern letters that seem to have been applied to the nation's newspapers as thoroughly as one might apply paint to the newsroom wall. We get very thoughtful, elaborate, and expensive portfolios. And we get everything in between. A person who wants the internship will write the essay. People who are too busy or who can't be bothered—well, that says something about their interest.
- Editors want to see how you write. Most clips are edited; most essays are not. That just makes sense. With clips only, editors are left to figure out the candidate's true writing ability.
- Just as the cover letter amplifies the résumé, the essay takes us beyond the letter. An essay is an exercise in judgment and creativity. Will your essay explore an incident that pushed you toward journalism, or is it a chronological recitation of your life? How readily do you recognize an interesting and relevant story? How do you tell it? Most importantly, editors want to know what motivates you, what your ambitions are, what you can contribute. An essay

The Edge

Before you list someone as a reference, ask them. But don't stop there, as most people will be polite and say yes. Ask them, "If I were to list you as a reference, what could you say about me?" If you like what you hear about yourself, then ask them to be references. If it doesn't sound too good, keep looking.

forces you to think about that and to explain the directions you'd like to pursue.

So, your essay should do two things. It should show what kind of writer you are, and it should show how journalism fits into the larger picture of your life.

A good essay shows how you, as a person, have become you, the journalist. It is evidence that your journalistic self is deeply rooted in the real you. It reflects how well you understand why you have applied for this internship. A bad essay is one in which the writing is lousy or pedestrian, or that fails to make the connection between you, as a person, and journalism, your passion.

When you write an essay about yourself, be yourself. Larding the essay up with all kinds of platitudes or clichés will not help you. Be honest, be yourself, be real.

Pay attention to putting a good lead on your essay. Do not be too concerned about when it should start. It could be at birth, but the parts of your life that are relevant to journalism most likely came later. Do not be afraid to project your desired future, your goals, and dreams. Do not be dull.

Essays can give editors insight into your motivations, and they can give you an opportunity to reflect seriously about your career choice and to focus your approach.

Guest: **Why we care so much about your essay**

By LINDA SHOCKLEY
Deputy Director
Dow Jones Newspaper Fund

Writing an essay is one of the most overlooked aspects of applying for an internship in the news business. The Dow Jones Newspaper Fund

The Edge ——————————————————————————————
Have essays, cover letters and résumés edited by the best copy editor you know. Don't ask a friend or a relative. Pay the copy editor to do a professional job. Saving you from even one gaffe can be worth the money.

places considerable emphasis on students' grades, practical journalistic experience, and the tests we devise and administer to potential hires.

But the essay, the original piece of writing submitted by reporting and editing candidates alike, is often the make-or-break document in the package. Why should so much pivot on one small part of the process? Because the essay is loaded with promises and predictors for future success. Evaluators want to learn what you think and what you think about. They need to know how effectively you communicate as a journalist without the filter of a copy desk.

The object is to win that coveted internship, so the essay demands care. Nothing says, "I don't care" like a sloppily written, disorganized collection of worn phrases. A rushed, typo-laden submission says you can't or don't manage your time effectively or write well under pressure.

Here are some tips.

Think about the topic and stay on it. You'll likely be asked to describe yourself as a journalist. What are your journalistic values? Don't veer off on a tangent about skiing. Use relevant anecdotes or examples to make your point.

Know yourself and your audience. Who are you? What's important to you and why? What have you already done and what would you like to do? Identifying for whom you are writing can make the difference between a contemporary, topical essay and a modern mystery. It's not a term paper. Citing Marshall McLuhan might be good for a mass media class, but not for this. And speaking of citing other sources. . .

Linda Shockley is deputy director of the Dow Jones Newspaper Fund, Inc., in Princeton, N.J., a non profit foundation at Dow Jones & Co., which promotes careers in journalism through internships, scholarships, and summer workshops. Shockley earned a bachelor's degree in journalism from the University of Bridgeport. Before joining the Newspaper Fund in 1988, she was an education reporter, news editor, bureau chief, columnist, and city editor for Gannett Suburban Newspapers in Westchester County, New York.

To thine own self be true. This is from Shakespeare, but is it Hamlet or MacBeth? If you're going to quote a passage from literature, the Bible, or anywhere else, verify its accuracy and the citation. Keep references—a dictionary, thesaurus, book of quotations—close by.

All by yourself. If it's not your original thought, attribute it. When plagiarism shows up it usually brings big problems along. Once I reviewed an essay full of much-too-familiar passages. It turned out the writer had borrowed liberally from Newspaper Fund career literature I had written. Needless to say, there were repercussions.

If it's trite, it's not right. Whether you really believe you were born "with ink in your veins," "a nose for news," or "wearing a green eyeshade," avoid these clichés like the plague. Imagine how many times recruiting editors have read them.

Writing is rewriting. Don't give your essay one pass. Start it, finish it, and put it aside. Then return to it. You'll probably see changes you'd like to make. Revise. Proofread. Read every word you've written, not the ones you thought you wrote.

When you are satisfied, print a final version. Make sure your name and relevant information are on each page. It sounds elementary but you'd be surprised how many candidates forget. ✻

Grades

The truth about your grade point average: Most newspaper editors will never ask for it.

Few editors and even fewer recruiters will ask for your transcript. Your grades make it or break it with colleges, scholarship programs, grad schools, and professional programs, but newspapers generally won't ask.

Why not? Two reasons.

One is that your grade point average is only one indicator of success and it is not as good an indicator of journalistic success as practical experience. While a good high school GPA might indicate how well you will do as an undergrad and a good undergrad GPA may tell us something about grad school, newsrooms are not classrooms. Editors use different criteria and indicators. Good grades can say that you're intelligent or work hard, but the editors are looking in different places for signs of that, too.

The second reason editors don't often ask about GPAs is we don't want you so wrapped up in raising them that you drop practical experience to do better on exams. Recruiters know that students talk to each other, and recruiters know that if they ask a couple students about their GPAs, students left and right will hear about it after the interview and some will start bailing out of activities—including journalism—to spend more time polishing their GPAs. That is not what we want.

Don't misunderstand. This is not an excuse to incinerate your GPA or to feel dejected because you worked hard to have a good one. Just remember to balance work in the classroom with work in a newsroom.

If you have a great GPA, crow about it. Put it on the résumé. Mention it in the interview. Get a tattoo. If it is OK and you're getting some great newsroom experience, that's good. If your GPA is in the toilet, don't mention it. Newsrooms don't want to hire dummies or slackers and they sometimes are the ones who wind up with the bad grades.

The key is balance. Do well in all areas—grades, journalism experience, leadership. Do not excel in just one area at the expense of the others. That will be true in your career, too.

Applying online

From the recruiters' little shop of horrors:

- Candidates who send two-sentence e-mails with a résumé and clips attached. The résumé does not open on the virus-protected office computer and the clips, sent as .pdf files or in some other graphical format, take up eight megabytes of space. For context, that is the size of two thousand short e-mails. This online application pushes the e-mail basket over its limit and cannot be answered until it is killed.
- The e-mailed résumé, with no note indicating why it has been sent. Is it for a particular position? Does the person want to work here? Did this get sent to just me, or a thousand people?
- The person who e-mails a thank-you and career update to several editors, including all their addresses, thereby telling all of them that he is keeping in touch with all the others.

So, how *does* one apply online?

First, recognize that e-mail is an additional tool, not a replacement. It complements letters, phone calls, face-to-face interviews, and faxes. It does not replace them. Before you hop online and start spewing application materials all over, think about the needs of your audience—hiring editors—and how best to meet those. If you show you are insensitive to the needs of the editor, he or she might reasonably conclude that you will not pay attention to the needs of your readers.

Six guidelines:

- Ask employers how they would like to receive information. If they ask you to e-mail a résumé, send it in.
- When possible, put your information in the body of the e-mail, in addition to sending it as an attached document. The information may look better in the attached documents, but some computer security systems discourage the opening of attachments.
- Create your documents in computer programs that are widely available. Word Perfect is one.
- Think about how the recipient will use your e-mail and choose a plan that will work well. Most people still apply on paper. That means that most of my files are on paper. Strange as it seems, if someone e-mails me a letter, résumé and ten clips digitally, I print all of that out to send copies to other editors or to start a file.
- Consider how your material will look on the receiving end. Whose printer do you trust more—yours or mine?
- Check your work before you hit send. E-mail is so instantaneous that people send e-mails with missing words—or intemperate ones—far more often than when they have to write a letter, print it out, find an envelope, address it, and stamp it. Those time-consuming steps give us the moments we sometimes need to cool down or check up.

4

The Interview

Interviewing is not as critical in the internship chase as it is in the job hunt, but get as many as you can. One good interview can put you ahead of the pack and every interview is good practice for the inevitable job interviews in your future.

Just making it to an interview can set you apart from other internship candidates, help you present yourself in depth, and let you learn more about the paper. You really should try to interview, if even just to practice. If you are not a strong interviewer and worry that it will hurt you, do it anyway. Prepare, practice, persist.

Intern candidates have four primary interview opportunities:

- Campus interviews
- Job fairs
- Interviews at the newspaper
- Telephone interviews

Each one requires different strategies.

Campus interviews

Take advantage of interview days arranged by your journalism department or career services office. In some law and business schools, students have to bid for interviews, "spending" points just to get in to see top recruiters. J-schools make things easier than that, so take advantage of these chances.

You'll find that the better J-schools get many more visits from recruiters. This is one of their selling points. These universities are on Main Street, using their students to attract recruiters and making their students eligible for more interviews. If your university is on Main Street, you have a real advantage. Use it.

Many universities discourage first- and second-year students from signing up for campus interviews. Some even forbid it. And some don't encourage students much beyond a single internship. These practices make life easier for career services, but they are not in your best interest.

Never be intimidated about being the youngest person on the interview roster. Recruiters may not hire the first-year student, but will come back the next year and say, "Didn't you interview with me when you were just starting? What's new with you now?"

One young man we hired at the *Free Press* said, "When I was a sophomore and no one would talk to me, you believed in me. How did you know?" The fact is, I believe in all the sophomores. It is as juniors and seniors that they begin to show me whether I was right.

Career services people are no different than you or me. They want life to be nice. Life is not nice if hordes of first- and second-year students are crowding seniors off the interview schedules. Seniors, who have invested way more time and money than younger students, feel entitled to interviews and opportunities. They also are sweating graduation. But guess what? Smart editors don't care. We want to talk to the best people, period. While some newspapers will consider only juniors and seniors, they'd rather meet a superior sophomore than a sleepy senior. If career services tells you this is simply not the case with one editor or another, listen. But know that it is not true with all of us.

If the interview gatekeepers at your school tell you that you're too young for internships, apply anyway. A sharp first-year student who catches the notice of a smart recruiter will be remembered. I keep lists of potential interns for three years into the future. You're never too young to apply. You may be too young to get, but you're never too young to try.

Work to get around rules that keep you out of campus interviews. Don't do it by being sneaky. Do it by being helpful and resourceful.

Here are some strategies:

Be nice to the gatekeepers. Do not be pushy or demanding. I ask career services people, profs, and secretaries about the students on my interview schedule. Often, they want to go over the list at lunch or at the end of the day. If you've spent two semesters being a pain in the place that these people sit on, I will hear about it. So, try to be nice.

Work career services as a good reporter works a beat. Show up. Ask around. Read the bulletin boards. Get to know the people. Be friend-ly and helpful. Take advice. Show them that you're serious. Become the first to find out when interviewers are coming. At some colleges, interview lists get filled up this way: Someone slaps a sign-up sheet on the wall or sends out e-mails and students claim slots, first-come, first-served. This happens because people in career services hate to tell tuition-paying students "Sorry, but we are giving these spots to bet-ter candidates." They would much rather say, "Oops, sorry! You're too slow," or, "Juniors and seniors, only!" No blame, no pain. Get into posi-tion to be first. Know when the sign-up opportunities are coming. At one university, the students who work in career services have inside access to the recruiters—and an on-site reference. Maybe that seems unfair.

Show up. So, OK, you worked career services like a beat and still didn't make the sign-up sheet. What now? On interview day, scrub be-hind your ears, put on your interview duds, and haunt career services. "Hey, if you come up with a no-show, just let me know, I'm ready as a fill-in." Smart career services people hate empty slots on the sched-ule even more than they hate letting in a sophomore. If a student suc-cumbs to nausea or nerves, career services is generally happy to throw any well-dressed student into the breech. This is classic being in the right place at the right time.

Be helpful. Does the editor need a ride from the airport? Carry-ing boxes? Setting up? Packing up at the end of the day? Touring the campus? I have seen students get time with recruiters all of these ways. (And one who offered to pick me up at the airport didn't even have a car. After she got the assignment, she mooched a car from a friend.) Have a copy of your résumé and clips with you, of course.

If the list has filled and your name is not on it, ask career services if the day can be extended. Sometimes, they call me about starting early or staying late for a good prospect. I usually say yes, but we all know this will work for only a few candidates a trip.

The Edge —————————————————————————————
Go into every job interview with three well thought-out questions.

Call the recruiter and ask to be put on the list. I frequently e-mail career services in advance and tell them which students I want to see. If I know of local people on the campus, good people I met on my last visit or whom I have seen elsewhere, I'll ask to interview them. Career services is there to help the editors and generally will make the arrangements the recruiter requests. In professional schools where students pay "points" to bid for interviews, the charge goes way down when recruiters make specific requests. I have had students who want to interview call me in advance.

Sometimes, students who have missed the list call me. I ask them why twenty other people got an appointment and they didn't. They had better have a good reason for missing and another one for why we should meet. Saying that the list filled up too fast is not a good reason. That tells me that the other twenty people I'm talking to are quicker. But I'll sometimes extend my stay for a couple candidates. It is difficult to add half a dozen to a schedule of fifteen or twenty people, and a half dozen additions means stretching an already long day by a couple hours. It is best to make that list.

Break the rules. You run the risk of being banned by career services, but consider whether and when to break the rules. Never lie to get a job interview, for heaven's sake, but know where you can push things. One morning, I interviewed students at Bowling Green State University in Ohio. In between morning and afternoon interviews, faculty members took me out to lunch and asked me what I thought of their students. I showed them one name on the list and said I liked his initiative. First one, and then all three profs said they did not know the young man. Then I told them: He was a student at the University of Toledo, from up the highway. He had heard there would be interviews on the nearby campus, drove down and signed up. Their first-come, first-served sign-up system had let in a student from another university.

Some candidates wonder whether it is better to go at the beginning of the day or the end. In my experience, it doesn't seem to make much difference either way, though I am always fresher in the morning than I am after I have done ten or twelve interviews. As a candidate, I would try for mornings with three things in mind:

- At what time of day are you at your best?
- Some people suggest the rules of primacy and recency—that people are more likely to remember things at the beginning or end.

This would suggest appointments at the start of the day, before or after lunch or at the end of the day.

- An interviewer can fall behind and cut late-day sessions short to make up the time. That is not going to happen to the first people on the schedule.

Really, though, I wouldn't get all in a bunch over interview order.

Remember that campus interviews and job fairs—in which an editor can talk to as many as twenty people in a day—are screening interviews. That implies we are trying to wind up with the best one or two people by screening out the rest. Getting the appointment is only the first part of the story. Being one of the best—or one who gets remembered for future opportunities—is the next part.

Job fairs

One of the most efficient tools recruiters use to meet a lot of talent in a little time is the job fair. Colleges organize them, some journalism associations have them at their conventions and individual newspapers or press associations organize them.

A job fair works like this: The organizers invite a bunch of recruiters and candidates to meet on the same day. This saves students the trouble of putting on the dog week after week, it gets all the students in one place for recruiters and it often attracts ancillary events such as training sessions or résumé-critique stations. The job fair happens in one or two big rooms filled with tables, one or two recruiters per table. Interviews may be pre-scheduled or open or a combination. With thirty recruiters doing twenty-minute interviews, it's possible to have six hundred interviews completed in one day. One reporter I know compared it to speed dating. Ick.

The Edge ————————————————————————

❝ Do look the interviewer in the eye. She or he wants to get to know you. She's trying to evaluate your potential, find out if you will work hard. ❞

—*Cheryl Butler, Washington Post recruiter, now retired*

Guest: **Preparing for the on-campus job fair**

By MELANIE HUFF
Assistant Dean of Students
Columbia Graduate School of Journalism

Whether it is a formal job interview or a more casual meeting at a job fair, it is important that you bear in mind that the only question an editor is looking to have answered is, "Can this person do the job I need to have done?" And contrary to what you may think, your objective isn't simply to convince the editor that you are the one who can do the job. What you want to do is to have a meaningful exchange that allows you both to determine if you are appropriate for this job and this paper.

The first indication that someone isn't ready for a particular position, even in the casual atmosphere of the job fair, is demonstrating a lack of professionalism. Arrive on time (if it is for a pre-scheduled appointment), in business attire, with your clips, résumé and references. Skip the t-shirt, gum and sloppy cup of coffee. Walk with confidence, look folks in the eye and offer a firm handshake.

In addition to professional behavior, you must be prepared to have an informed discussion. For a regular job interview, you generally will be able to spend some time learning about the paper, the issues in the region and the demographics. At a job fair, this level of preparation is neither feasible nor expected, as you will be meeting with people from many papers and you may not even know in advance which news organizations will be attending.

Melanie Huff, assistant dean of students at the Columbia University Graduate School of Journalism, has been with the school since the fall of 1987. Prior to joining the Dean of Students office, she ran the Office of Career Services for many years. She has a bachelor of arts from Barnard College and a master's degree from Columbia University Teachers College. She serves as a writing coach with Legal Outreach and as a convention coordinator for the South Asian Journalists Association.

However, this does not mean you should go in without some prep work. These interactions can form the basis for follow-up correspondence and hopefully another meeting for a more formal interview, so you want to make the most of them.

Your best bet when faced with multiple interactions is to be prepared to discuss your commitment to journalism, your news philosophy, and what you are qualified to do.

You should know in advance how you will answer the most standard questions asked of applicants. For example: Why do you want to be a journalist? Why reporting? Why editing? What stories would you like to cover? Why will you make a successful journalist? What is the best story you have ever written and why? Give me an example of a story you think you handled very well. Give me an example of a story you wished you had covered differently and how would you cover it now? When asked a question you have not thought before, don't be afraid to pause and think about your reply.

You must also be able to verbalize your belief in your journalism skills. This doesn't mean portraying yourself as God's gift to journalism, but it does mean that you need to demonstrate that you know that you have what it takes. People who are reticent about their abilities often have difficulty in landing jobs, even if they are qualified.

Young people eager to secure employment often forget that this process isn't just about getting a job; it is about getting the right job. Having questions prepared in advance for the interviewer will allow you to learn if this is a place where you really want to work. Your questions could include: Are beats divided up geographically or by topic? How much feedback do reporters get from editors? What is the person who had this job previously doing now? Why is your paper a good one at which to begin my career? Remember that asking only about vacations and benefits suggests that you aren't really interested in the work.

Finally, don't forget the thank-you note. It is a chance to remind the interviewer of who you are and what you discussed. You will be one among many people with whom the interviewer met that day. It also gives you the opportunity to bring up anything that didn't come up in the meeting that will strengthen your candidacy. ✴

Beating the job-fair jitters

While some people like the hustle and bustle of a job fair, others find it overwhelming to walk into a room with all that activity and, right down the line, see the *Times,* the *Post,* the *Tribune,* the *Register,* and the *Press,* all interviewing simultaneously. Their friends, dressed in stiff clothes and sweating, stand in little queues, clip packages in arms. Interviews happen elbow to elbow with very little privacy. Some feel like they're in a meat market.

People who hate job fairs tend to feel they are artificial. They don't like "schmoozing," "working the room," or "playing the game." They feel like job fair roadkill, run over by smooth, socially savvy students who suck up all the interviews, even though they may be evenly matched, journalistically.

In either case, a job fair can be an ideal opportunity for pursuing an internship or job, so you want to take advantage of it. Here are some strategies for making the most of a job fair.

Prepare

Have plenty of copies of your résumé and work samples. While the job fair organizers might be distributing copies of participants' résumés, it pays to have your own just in case. You don't want to be caught without and you don't want to leave the job fair, where every minute can count, to feed paper into a copy machine.

Have realistic expectations

Few people will walk away from a day of interviews with a job offer. The world doesn't work that way. Smart people will be satisfied with a few promising leads, a professional who shows a willingness to help and useful information from a workshop. If you leave with that much, you have spent your time well. When you talk to a dozen recruiters in a day, expect a few to be duds. Don't let them get into your head or in your way.

Do your homework

If you plan to interview with a particular newspaper, learn about it. Know where it is, its circulation, publishing cycle, and position in its market. What is the competition? Who owns it? Who is the editor? Check it out on the Web. Be ready to ask some informed questions. Some recruiters like to ask, "What can you tell me about my newspaper?" What they want to know is whether you have any desire to live in that area or whether you've done any homework. Show them.

Dress to impress

You don't have to be haute couture to be a hot commodity, but you should show the recruiter that you're aware of what people are wearing in offices these days. For women, I suggest a business suit or a dress or skirt of a professional length. Blouses should be long enough that they need to be tucked in. Waist-baring styles do women no favors. Most of your peers will be wearing closed-toe shoes and nylons. For men, I suggest office attire. Most of your peers will be wearing suits or jackets and ties. Concerned that the dress code in corporate America will squash your identity? Let's hope that your identity has more to it than a style of dress. But if you feel strongly that an earring (or several), or a mode of dress is an important part of who you are, then stick with it. Understand, though, that this might cost you a job with certain places—places where you might not really want to work, anyway. Ethnic clothing or hairstyles, or clothing worn for religious reasons, is appropriate in most metro newsrooms, but editors may evaluate your look in the light of what they perceive to be standards in the community. Tight, revealing, or out-and-out sloppy clothing is not going to make the right kind of statement.

Break down the job fair to put it on manageable terms

Approach the job fair one interview at a time. You are not on display in front of all these people. After all, they are busy doing their own interviews. They are not all looking at you; they are thinking about what they have to do. During your interview, the job fair becomes just two people—you and the interviewer. Hear just what he or she is saying. Don't be distracted by the sideshow going on around you. It is not important. All that matters—and it matters just for the time you are there—is what happens in the six-foot circle around you and the recruiter. Just as good recruiters try to create tiny pools of listening and attention inside noisy job fairs, you should isolate the interview space as a tiny pool that you can easily manage.

Sometimes, a person walking behind you will catch the recruiter's eye and he or she will look behind you. Although good interviewers try to avoid distractions, it's difficult because, in addition to interviewing you, they have to manage people waiting to come after you. Don't take these distractions and interruptions personally. Shrug them off and stay focused on answering the questions and pushing your points across.

Be outgoing

Talk to recruiters and other job-seekers whenever you have the chance. You can do a lot of good work at meals, breaks and workshops. If you are with friends, split up. You can talk later. Don't use time you could spend networking by huddling together. You miss opportunities and look insecure. (On a couple of occasions, friends or lovers have come to my job-fair table together. Never do this.)

Wear your nametag

Have your name on wherever you are likely to encounter others from the job fair—even elsewhere in the building or on the street around the job fair. Nametags make us feel conspicuous, I know. But that's good. You came to the job fair to be conspicuous.

Be assertive

If you want to talk to a particular paper but are not scheduled to, find the recruiter at a spare, early moment and set up a meeting. Don't let a representative for the newspaper of your dreams come within ten feet of you and then get away. The way you handle this situation indicates the kind of journalist you are.

Be open-minded

You never really considered working at a newspaper with a circulation of less than 100,000? Well, you should. Those are the papers where most people work and where nearly everyone starts. Besides, they can be huge fun and great places to learn. I once started chatting with a student who had no intention of coming to my newspaper and told me so. She was going to go to *People* magazine. Her mind changed over the next few months and she asked to come to the *Free Press*. We hired her and by the end of the next summer she had been named intern of the year.

The Edge ───

Editors think that the people most likely to complain about a new job are those who complain about their previous one. So, don't.

Make a personal connection
Job-fair recruiters interview twenty people in a day. Only a few will
stand out. You'll have a better chance of that if you engage in a conversation that goes beyond the superficial. Take a chance by revealing
something about your career motivations. Ask questions that mean
something to you. Draw out the recruiters' experiences and advice.

Follow up
The people who get the most out of job fairs are the ones who do the
most after job fairs. Follow up with a letter, phone call, or e-mail. Job-
seekers who think that the work stops when the job fair stops are the
ones who have the most trouble getting their careers started.

Guest: Beyond the job fair

By RAY MARCANO
Internet General Manager
Cox Ohio Publishing

After decades of minority jobs fairs, initiatives to further diversify
newsrooms and scholarship programs aimed at journalists of color, we
all know the obvious—newspaper companies have set diversity as a
primary business objective.

We also know that, by and large, those initiatives have not worked
as well as newspapers have hoped. The 2007 study by the American
Society of Newspaper Editors found:

- The percentage of women in daily newsrooms was about 37 percent
- Women represented 37.56 percent of newsroom supervisors
- About 13.62 percent of the newsroom staffers were minorities,
  while the Census Bureau reports that about 37 percent of the nation's people belong to minority groups.
- Minorities account for just 10.9 percent of the total number of
  newsroom supervisors.
- 392 newspapers employed no minorities

Despite all of the initiatives, it could be we're not focusing on the one
way that could really drive newsroom diversity.

We know about the social case for diversity: It's important to have a newsroom that reflects the community a newspaper serves. That way, you have different ranges of experiences, from class to gender to color. And it makes newsrooms richer. That's why someone like me—born of an African-American mother and Puerto Rican father in the slums of the South Bronx—has different experiences than someone who was raised in a picket-fenced home in the suburbs.

There's also the business reason to diversify. In order to make money and increase profits, businesses have to reach out to all segments of the community. Otherwise, various groups are bound to ask: Why don't I see people who look like me?

But true diversity goes beyond what happens within the borders of our newsroom. It goes beyond our employer-mandated goals.

For true diversity to work, individuals have to buy into the concept —not through company pontification or via an employee handbook. And that's the area that has, by and large, lacked focus.

It's one thing to attend job fairs and assist in the hiring of a woman or a minority. It's quite another to spend time with the people who are nothing like you.

People tend to go home to areas in which their neighbors are just like them. They don't spend time understanding the cultures and values of people from which they differ.

For example, an Ohio State University study showed that students in a diverse school were most likely to choose friends of the same race.

It isn't that people have to attain deep friendships with different races, genders, or cultures. But they can make a difference by simply

Ray Marcano is Internet general manager of Cox Ohio Publishing. He has held a number of management jobs in his twenty-two years at the Dayton (Ohio) Daily News, including sports editor, metro editor, regional editor, and deputy managing editor. He began his reporting career in New York City, his hometown, and has also worked at newspapers in Oklahoma. He is the former national president of the Society of Professional Journalists, the nation's largest journalism association, has been accepted into the Fulbright Senior Specialist program, and chairs the new technology committee for the Ohio Newspaper Association.

being acquaintances. They can make a difference by:

- Taking someone not like you to lunch, or doing something as simple as having a beer after work with that person.
- Attending a different church, even if just for one Sunday, to get a feel for the differences in worship.
- Forming discussion groups for periodic meetings to discuss differences in culture and gender.

There's another critical component to diversity that's often overlooked: whites, especially white males, must play an active role in order for real diversity to be successful.

Matters of diversity seem to be couched in minority terms, with the emphasis on people of color. Soni (2000) and others note that most diversity initiatives are designed for women and minorities since those are the excluded groups that have suffered from an historic lack of opportunity.

But such programs fail to acknowledge that not all whites come from privilege, and the Appalachian culture is as rich as that of women, blacks, Hispanics, Asians, and other ethnic groups.

Embracing diversity won't happen simply as a result of corporate fiat. It has to become a way of life. ✳

Sources:
Soni, V. (2000, September/October). A twenty-first century reception for diversity in the public sector: A case study. Public Record Administration Review, 60, 395-408
ASNE diversity: http://www.asne.org/index.cfm?id=3432
Ohio State University study: http://researchnews.osu.edu/archive/frndseg.htm

Interviewing at the newspaper

Sometimes, you can snag an internship interview right at the newspaper. Some guidelines:

- Interview with the right person. If you want an internship, ask who makes the decision and try to talk with that person. An interview with almost the right person is almost good.
- Get in before the internship application deadline. Is it after the deadline? Remember that while January may be one month after the deadline, it is likely that not all offers have been made, and being a month late for one cycle may mean being eleven months

early for the next. One intern candidate made an appointment to come to see me—for the day the rejection letters were being mailed out.

- Try to extend your interview visit and meet more people by scheduling it near one of the daily news meetings that all newspapers have. Ask if you can sit in on that meeting.
- Do everything you would for an on-campus or job fair interview, including some prepared questions and good follow-up.

When I travel, I often take an extra day to see people working in that city. I maintain lists of candidates organized by cities I regularly visit such as Chicago, New York, Washington, and San Francisco. I keep similar lists according to college campuses. In this way, I can add half a dozen interviews to a business trip. Steal my strategy. If you're going someplace, check the *Editor & Publisher Year Book* to see which newspapers are in that area. Call the internship coordinators and ask if you can come in for an interview.

Guest: Combining visits with vacations

By KATHLEEN L. PELLEGRINO
Recruitment Editor and Staff Attorney
South Florida Sun-Sentinel

Using a vacation trip to make contacts with a potential employer is a great way to position yourself for a job offer.

We encourage vacationing journalists to visit our newsroom and several of those who've done so later joined our staff.

Here are some pointers if you would like to try this:

- Make arrangements about a month in advance; don't just show up.

The Edge ――――――――――――――――――――――――――――――
Most newspapers publish in the morning and typically have a morning news meetings around 11 a.m. and an afternoon news meeting around 3 p.m.

- Start with the recruiter, and if there isn't one or you don't get a response, try the editor whose area you would like to work in. This is a free interview opportunity for the newspaper and someone will take advantage.
- Don't waste people's time by asking for directions. Show how self-sufficient you are by finding your way. Do ask about parking or security so you can leave extra time if needed.
- Don't be late. But if your plane is delayed, advise the person you are meeting.
- Leave time between your arrival in the city and the interview to read that day's paper.
- Be flexible. Don't tell the interviewer that you have only a half-hour because your ride is waiting. If the person likes you, he or she may want you to meet other editors.
- If you pay for parking, a taxi or anything else, don't ask or expect to be reimbursed.
- Provide a résumé and clips in advance and bring several extra sets with you. If you are underqualified for the paper, be upfront about it and address it in a cover letter. Make it clear that you would like an informational interview and the chance to get advice and make contacts for future possibilities.
- The Internet means there's no excuse for you not having some idea about the issues of the area you are visiting and background on the paper. Working such information into an interview or mentioning that you've monitored the Web site wins big points with editors.
- Don't use a trip paid for by one employer to visit the competitor.

Kathleen Pellegrino is recruitment editor and staff attorney for the South Florida Sun-Sentinel in Fort Lauderdale, Florida. At that newspaper, she has also worked as an assistant city editor and a metro reporter.

- Don't show up in flip-flops and a sundress. While you don't need to be interview-suit formal, be professional.
- Assume that you will know someone or someone will know you in the newsroom you visit. So even though it is not a formal job interview, evaluate in advance whether to address this with your current employer.

Making time for an informational interview while traveling is a great way to check out a potential employer and make a personal impression that you can't make with only a résumé and clips. ✳

Telephone interviews

Intern candidates usually congregate in much larger pools than job candidates. A large newspaper may get as many as six hundred applications for internships but only a couple dozen for a job. The intern pool is often broad, with applications from across the country and around the world.

Because internships are ten- to twelve-week positions, few newspapers go to the expense of bringing in candidates for interviews. The *Boston Globe* does, but that is an exception. If the newspaper is interested in a distant candidate, it may ask for a telephone interview. You can certainly offer to do a phone interview with a distant paper.

Here's how to prepare for a telephone interview:

- If you get a surprise call from an editor who wants to interview you right now, graciously ask to set up a time—soon. Editors requesting phone interviews are probably at the finalist stage and itching to make offers, so don't put them off for more than a day.
- Set the interview up so it can occur over a land line from a place where you can close the door and shut out distractions. Be very clear on the time of the interview, especially if you are in different time zones. You don't want to be an hour late for your interview because someone was confused.
- Prepare for the phone interview as you would for a face-to-face interview. Read up on the latest issues of the newspaper, its ownership, management team, and reasons it has recently been in the news.
- For the interview, have:

- ➤ A copy of your résumé
- ➤ Printouts of relevant Web pages from the newspaper's site (that day's top stories, the staff list, a company history)
- ➤ A few good questions
- ➤ The correct pronunciation of the editor's name written on a piece of paper if it is tricky.
- ➤ A glass of water
- Be at your phone fifteen minutes early, just as you would be for a face-to-face interview.
- As odd as it might seem, dress professionally for the interview. That will help you interview more professionally.
- Sit up straight or even stand during the interview. You'll feel more confident and that will come across in your voice.
- Turn off distractions, such as your cell phone or the call-waiting feature on the phone you're using.
- Without body language or facial expressions to read the editor's mood or to communicate your own, place more emphasis in communicating with words: "Did I answer your question?" "Would you like an example of that?" "Let me make sure I understand the question …" "That's a good question." "This is an exciting opportunity. I really hope this works out."

E-mail inquiries

Rarely, you may get something that looks like an e-mail interview. It is a list of questions. These are, for any journalist or hiring manager, vastly second-rate to face-to-face interviews or telephone interviews. Yet, they happen.

Answer them:

- Promptly
- With perfect spelling, grammar, usage, and punctuation. Do not treat an e-mail interview as informally as you would treat an on-

---

❝Anticipate questions. Don't be caught fumbling. Feel free to ask as well as answer questions. The best question: Why would I want to work for your paper?❞

—*Cheryl Butler, Washington Post recruiter, now retired*

line chat with your friend.
- Keep your answers succinct, but use them to show that you can write.
- Feel free to add a couple—but just a couple—questions of your own to the end. Good questions make you seem curious. Twenty questions make you seem odd.

One of the great weaknesses of so-called e-mail interviews is that the subject of the interview can call in other people to help frame and edit the answers. Take advantage of this by thinking your answers through and editing them well or asking someone to look them over before you press SEND.

Guest: Know it all

By REGINALD STUART
Corporate Recruiter
The McClatchy Company

When recruiters interview prospects for full-time jobs and internships, they try to assess the likely compatibility between the potential employer and prospective employee. It's not a precise science, but the responses help both parties decide what steps to take next.

For almost every prospect, there is a standard line of questions, many of which have already been answered on the candidate's resume: education, skills, work experiences. Then comes the stumper: What do you know about our company?

It's amazing how many otherwise composed and energized prospects suddenly melt into embarrassment and then deliver a series of disconnected, generic answers:

"Your company is a major printer of newspapers," says one. "You are a major publishing company," offers another prospect. "I know you have papers in a lot of cities," says another.

Before that stumper question, the prospect would have had the interviewer believe that he or she knew it all. At this point, the ship wrecked.

As countless job seekers have heard from me, the one phrase to learn early in one's career and to retain for use throughout one's life is: "I don't know."

"I don't know" is commonly associated with being ignorant. No problem. If you are ignorant on a topic, you are. Fess up that you don't know so that someone who does can help you.

Don't be embarrassed. Use that phrase whenever it is needed. It's far better than rolling your eyes away from the interviewer and mumbling some useless phrases. Put "I don't know" out there so the conversation can quickly move on. You'll rebound faster and get more from your conversation than if you try to bluff your way through.

A former colleague, oft times characterized as a smart dumb blonde, used that phrase all the time in her reporting. She had no problem telling people "I don't know anything about this. Can you help me?" As a result, she got more detail, more inside information, more Page One stories.

Afraid to take this approach to self-enlightenment?

Get in front of a mirror and say it to yourself in ways that allow you to be comfortable when you have to say it in public. It's one of the best skills you'll have in your tool bag.

Over time, saying "I don't know," will help you learn a lot more about a lot more. While some people who know, and many who don't, will ridicule you as dumb or stupid, you'll have enough confidence not to be distracted.

Early in the first United States war against Iraq, a young reporter for *The Washington Post* was sent to a military press briefing. He had no military experience and had not been to the War College where he could learn military terms, jargon, and strategy.

Reginald Stuart, corporate recruiter for The Mc-Clatchy Company, has been a journalist for nearly four decades, having worked for The Nashville Tennessean, General Electric Broadcasting, The New York Times, Philadelphia Daily News and Knight Ridder. Stuart is a graduate of Tennessee State University and Columbia University in the City of New York. He has won several awards for journalism. He has also received honors for service to the profession, including the Wells Memorial Key, Ida B. Wells Award, Robert Maynard Legend Award and the Asian American Journalists Association's Leadership in Diversity Award.

Participating in a briefing was one way to help him get his feet wet. When he began asking questions any pedestrian would ask, his colleagues began to wonder aloud why this reporter was there and to complain about how "dumb" his questions were.

The rookie reporter held his ground until he understood what was being said. By asking such "stupid" questions, he got answers that opened everyone's eyes.

Regardless of one's standing in life—age, education, region of the country, or breadth of experiences—it's impossible for one person to know it all. It would be helpful for a job seeker to know more details than a few generic phrases. If you want to work for a company, do some detailed reading on the company before you interview. Know some intimate details about what it does and what you like about it. Know enough to make the recruiter say: "I didn't know that!"

As you navigate life, keep that "I don't know" handy. You will gain more respect from people because you really will know. You may not know it all, but you'll know a lot more than if you gave the bluff only to be found out. Remember, knowing is half the battle. It certainly helps you get a job and keep a job. ✳

Follow-ups

Since my first year recruiting, I have written thank-you notes to almost everyone I have interviewed at a convention, job fair or college campus. I began with typed letters that were all basically the same. I soon switched to handwritten cards. I have sent thousands.

My handwriting is not that clear, even on a good day, and when I have to sit down and write twenty-five at a crack, it is even worse. But I am not trying to win a prize for penmanship. I am trying to make an impression. I know that few other recruiters will make the time to personally thank people for interviewing. The note makes my newspaper stand out, it recognizes that everyone's time is valuable, it reinforces a point from our interview, it keeps the door open and it sends a message. The message is: Follow-up notes are effective; try them yourself.

Very few interviews lead to internships. More often, during a long day of interviewing candidates, I eliminate many more candidates than I advance. But good follow-up can lead to something down the road. One reason I write follow-up notes and try to be sensitive with rejection letters is that I know I am communicating with dozens of people who, while they might not be chosen for the internship of the moment, are people I want to encourage for future opportunities.

Take the long view.

5

Negotiation and Rejection

With internships, there is very little room for negotiation. Because an internship is one of your first opportunities to handle a job offer, though, it is a first chance to start learning how to negotiate. This will help you later. Some journalists are notoriously bad negotiators. They ask for nothing or they ask for everything. You likely will not feel very powerful as an internship candidate, but the fact that you get an offer shows you have something that editors want. That shows you have value, and value is the basis for negotiating.

Interns typically have no wiggle room on wages, no health plan and if there are any fringe benefits, they will be the same for every intern. You may be able to negotiate your start date, specific days you will need off and, perhaps—perhaps—aspects of your assignment.

The trickiest internship negotiations come if you have the good fortune to get more than one offer and must navigate among competing offers. Before we get to that, let's talk about handling the simpler and more common situation: the single offer. We'll start with one of my favorite intern negotiations.

Handling the single offer

I called a student with an internship offer and instantly regretted it. He was soon asking whether I thought my offer was as good as one he hoped to get from the Associated Press for an internship in a city where his girlfriend lived, or a spot he might get in the MetPro program.

It was clear he was not as excited about us as I had been about him. As we talked, I could feel this prospect slipping away. In fact, I was hoping for it. Thankfully, he declined. Before my phone cooled off, I was punching numbers on my next candidate.

No hemming with this one, and no hawing. As soon as the offer was out of my mouth, she was hooting in my ear: "Yes! Yes! I accept! I accept!"

I really like that kind of enthusiasm, but I said, "Listen, when someone makes you an offer, be excited, be enthusiastic, but ask for a little time to think about it. There's nothing wrong with that and it's good practice. Tell you what: I won't accept your acceptance. Think about this overnight. Talk to the people you count on, your professors and family. Maybe you'll have some questions. At least think of some questions. Let's talk tomorrow."

She agreed.

As soon as I got into the newsroom the next morning, my phone rang.

I picked it up. "Hello?"

"I accept!"

Sigh. "OK, you're in. But don't you have any questions at all?"

"Oh. Yes … is it paid?"

Though I didn't think much of the negotiating, you can't beat *The* enthusiasm. She did a great job with us and ultimately went on to the *Washington Post,* where, after reporting in Iraq, she was named the National Association of Black Journalists' young journalist of the year. She is Theola Labbé, and you can find her advice on Page 143.

When someone makes an offer, they open a window. This is your negotiating time. That window stays open until the offer is accepted, rejected or—rarely—withdrawn.

When you negotiate a start date, get there as soon as you can. Try to be one of the first to get to the newspaper, to learn its culture and its ways of doing things. You'll catch more assignments as one of the few than you will as one of the many. You could become the one who shows the other interns how to operate. Editors like to see helpfulness in a staff member.

If there turns out to be money in the budget to extend some interns, the editors will follow four considerations:

- Who is doing a good job?
- Who can stay longer?
- How long can they stay?
- Who will reach the end of their prescribed time first?

So, the sooner you start and the better you do, the more likely you are to get extra weeks, extra work, and extra pay. If you are one of the last to start, you'll also be one of the last to be considered for an extension. Money for extensions could run out. They won't know you as well as they know people who started a month earlier. If you're returning to school at the same time as everyone else, you simply might not have any free weeks at the end of the internship season. Having your internship extended is impressive résumé material. No one cares when you say, "I *would* have been extended, except that. . ."

If you need special days off for the marriage of a friend or Granny's 100th birthday, ask for those days during your negotiating window. Do not procrastinate until "the right time" to ask. The sooner you ask, the easier it is for editors to plan. Although it might seem hard to ask, it only gets harder if you wait. Ask early, and you'll probably find that it is no big deal. Do not expect to get paid for your days away, but do ask for the chance to make up the time later. You didn't sweat to land a ten- or twelve-week internship and then miss the full benefit—and earnings—of that experience.

Don't ask to have work scheduled around activities that might seem to the editor to be inconsequential. You want to show that doing great work is your top priority. Treat your internship like a job. We do.

You may be able to negotiate some enhancements to your work experience. If you're a copy editor who wants to spend a week in graphics or a reporter who wants to do a ride-along with a photographer, ask. Some small- and mid-size newspapers construct internships where people rotate through several departments. If that doesn't suit you, ask about that. It's unusual for a newspaper that is all the way at one end of the concentrate-or-rotate spectrum to move all the way to the other end, but there are many points in between.

Never try to negotiate everything just to see what you can get. Negotiation implies some reluctance, that you might not accept the position. If you try to negotiate everything, you'll come off as less interested in the position. Cool, calculating candidates who seem interested only in what they can get send signals that they are not very passionate about what they will do. That is no way to walk into an internship or a job.

One grad weighing offers from us and another newspaper asked if we would increase the salary. We couldn't because she was coming into a program with a set rate that would be unfair to vary from person to person. I also knew that the other newspaper would offer her less money, but when I asked her how much they were offering, she didn't even know. She wasn't saying we were low; she just wanted to see if we would go higher. We couldn't. She immediately agreed to come, anyway. There was no real harm done and she started on a good note at a fair rate.

Get it in writing

After you have reached a verbal agreement on the internship, ask for a letter outlining the offer. Some companies call this the offer letter. If the company asks why you want it in writing, say that you just want to be clear on what you and the editor have agreed to. If the editor says, "we don't send out contracts, we keep our word," reassure the editor that it's not a matter of trust and that you keep your word, too, but that you just want the details spelled out so you know what you've agreed to.

Check the offer letter over. If it omits anything, correspond by e-mail so that you can quickly get the missing details in writing. This will protect you in the common occurrence that the person you negotiated with does not wind up being the same person you work for. At large newspapers, internship offers are often made by recruiters who do not directly supervise the interns; at any paper, turnover can mean the person you work for is not the one who hired you months before the internship started.

Asking for written offers is more important with jobs, so asking for them with internships is kind of like practice.

You may find that your first internship offer comes from one of your "safety" papers and that you don't want to accept it. Declining without burning a bridge requires finesse, but it is not really negotiating.

Juggling simultaneous offers

If you have enough talent, connections or luck to get more than one offer at the same time, you'll have to choose. During internship-offer season, the best and luckiest can get offers within hours of each other. Some offers arrive just hours after candidates commit to someone else.

For most, one offer is fortune enough and the only way that there might be more than one at a time is if they get busy and shake the bushes a little.

Because hundreds of internship offers drop in the space of just a few months and because so many candidates send mass applications, you could face a negotiation challenge at internship time that you will never see again in your career.

When you get your first offer, the clock starts ticking.

Here's how to use this window to negotiate among offers.

First, enthusiastically thank the editor who made the offer, but do not commit. Whether you ultimately accept this internship or not, this is the newspaper that told you your long search has succeeded. You will be working somewhere. You should express your gratitude—and then get as many details about the offer as you can.

Negotiate the amount of time you have to decide, unless this is one of your top-choice newspapers. What is a fair amount of time? Any reasonable editor should give you a couple of days to think over an offer. A week is generous. If you ask for more than a week, your hidden message is, "I'm not really excited about this offer, but if I'm desperate, I'll take it." This phone call may be your first step in establishing an important relationship. Some editors demand an answer right away. The most severe was an editor who told the candidate that the offer would go away when he hung up the phone. That is extreme and unusual—but it can happen.

Once you have established a deadline with the editor who made the offer, call the newspapers you're more interested in, explain that you have an offer on the table and ask them where they are in their selection process. Call only the newspapers you prefer to the one that made the offer and where you think you have a decent chance. Imagine how dumb you would sound if you called a newspaper, said that you had an offer somewhere else and, when the second newspaper also made an offer, you said, "No, thanks!"

Be careful with these calls. You don't want to come across as a player. This can happen if editors compare notes. That is more likely to happen if the newspapers you're calling are owned by the same company. Even if they're not, there are lots of hidden, informal networks among editors.

One corporate recruiter who worked with dozens of newspapers found that several of his newspapers were jockeying for a candidate he had been promoting. The recruiter came to believe the student was playing the editors against each other. The recruiter went from promoting the guy to wanting to have nothing to do with him. He told the candidate—and he told the editors.

Never, ever falsely imply that you have an offer from one paper to draw out an offer from another. It is dishonest and it can be dangerous. Recruiters and internship coordinators know each other and, although we are guarded, we do talk. If two editors get to talking after the interns are selected and discover that someone has lied, that person's credibility is shot. This news will travel fast and it will dog you.

As you call papers and explain the situation, you're likely to get one of four answers. Here they are, and this is what they mean:

- "Well, we want to make an offer, too." You now have two offers, Get all the information you can about this one to make a decision. If you've started with your top choices, you can stop calling papers and will soon have to turn down the original offer.
- "OK, we're very interested in you, too. We'll get back to you." This is difficult. Press them for an answer before the first's paper's deadline and ask when you can get details. Until you have a firm offer, though, don't stop trying.
- "Congratulations. That's a good offer. If I were you, I'd take it." Between the lines, the editor is telling you that an offer is unlikely.
- "It's too early. We will not have a decision in time for your deadline." This is a gamble. If you want to hold out for this paper, passing up other offers, ask what your chances are and when the decision will come.

This period of checking with your other newspapers can be very stressful. You don't have a lot of time and you have to find several editors and pressure them.

> ### JobsPage in My Pocket
> Questions to ask about an internship offer
> - What is the position?
> - What would my responsibilities be?
> - Where would I work?
> - How long is the internship?
> - When would I start?
> - How much does it pay?
> - What kind of help is offered to find housing?
> - Can I get contact information for people who had this internship last year?
> - When does the newspaper need an answer?

If you're lucky, one of your favorites will make an offer. It gets awkward when a hoped-for paper tells you that it is not close to decision time and can't even tell you how good your chances are. You'll have to let those papers go or gamble and wait. If you decide to wait, tell the slow paper that's what you're doing so they don't assume you took the early offer and drop you from their list.

If you wind up with more than one offer, get as many facts on the table as you can in the first calls. It will save you from making second calls. The JobsPage in My Pocket on Page 97 that can help you look at the facts. Some people make decisions with lists of pluses and minuses, others go with their feelings and most use a combination.

If you can't shake out any more offers, get ready to accept the original offer with grace, enthusiasm and gratitude.

Guest: Picking the right offer

By RANDY HAGIHARA
Senior Editor for Recruitment
The Los Angeles Times

You might think it's pure agony—trying to decide which of several job offers to take. Everyone should be so lucky. Having options is always a good thing. Having no options is the real agony.

In the event you're faced with the prospect of picking from among several offers—whether it's a job or an internship—here are a few tips to consider:

1) Figure out what's most important to you. Money might be a factor, but the quality of the job or the chance for advancement might

Randy Hagihara is senior editor for recruitment and director of the summer internship program at the Los Angeles Times. He has worked at a number of other California newspapers, including the San Jose Mercury News, the Oakland Tribune, and the Peninsula Times Tribune in Palo Alto. A native of Los Angeles, he attended Cal State Northridge and Los Angeles Trade Technical College.

be even more important. The size of the paper might be alluring, but bigger doesn't always translate into better. 2) If you're given some time to make a decision, use it to do your reporting. That means talking to people who work at the newspapers making the offers and, if you can track them down, some people who have left. Ask a lot of questions of the editors. What kind of assignments will you be doing? What kind of editing will you receive? What kind of opportunities are there for development? 3) Trust your gut instincts. You can weigh the pros and cons of each offer till you're blue in the face, but in the end, you might find your reasoning merely muddled or blurred.

If you receive an offer but are under serious consideration elsewhere, try to buy some time. I make it a personal policy to be as upfront as possible. Explain your situation to the editor making the offer and ask if you can have some time to decide. Be careful, however: You don't want to sound ungrateful or like you're playing off one offer to get another. Most editors are reasonable people. But if it's an internship you're being offered, don't be surprised if the editor wants your answer on the spot, in which case I'd accept and be happy about it.

Finally, after you've made your decision, don't bother looking back at what might have been. A life of regret is a life of frustration. Always keep looking forward, even if you come to realize you may have made the wrong choice. Make the most of the experience. A positive attitude can help you overcome any number of seemingly insurmountable hurdles. I've made a few career decisions that might have seemed rather foolish at the time, but in the end they helped me get to where I wanted to go. ✺

Pressure tactics

Why do newspapers put so much pressure on internship candidates?

Remember, scores of newspapers make hundreds of similar offers to the same pool of people in a short period. That does not happen with jobs. We editors know that you, the internship candidate, have a lot riding on this sweepstakes, but we feel pressure, too. We want to get the best people we can and the competition can make us get aggressive. We know that if our top prospects ask for time to decide, they might use that time to attract other offers and that our next-best candidates could get signed while we are waiting. We don't like to lose our first

Weight each variable 0-4, with four meaning most important and zero meaning not important. If pay matters a lot to you but the social scene does not, multiply the pay ranking by four and social scene by one or zero. Then rank the papers on each variable, giving more points to the paper that is better on that variable. If you are comparing two papers, the top ranking is two points. If you are comparing three, the best paper gets three points. If factors are pretty much the same at both jobs or you gave that factor a ranking of zero, just skip that line. Multiply the weights by the rankings and total.

Variables	Weight 0-4	Newspaper A (Reverse rank)	Newspaper B (Reverse rank)	Newspaper C (Reverse rank)
Weekly take-home pay (after taxes)				
Circulation size				
Quality/reputation				
Ownership				
Assignment				
Vibe				
Training				
Location				
Social scene				
Transportation				
TOTALS				

choice—and then choices two, three, and four.

Although it seems editors hold all the cards, we don't always feel that way. One grad was negotiating with two of the nation's largest newspapers. Both papers are filled with talent. The recruiter at the losing newspaper referred to the recent grad, who was in her very early twenties, as "a shark." The candidate, though, felt more like a guppy.

I once made an offer to a person for a position in a specialized program. She thanked me, asked for time to decide, and called back in a week to say she had come up with the identical offer from another newspaper—*The Washington Post*. She went with *The Post* and it hired her after the internship. I know that a shorter decision window might have prevented that—and that other candidates could have made commitments while I was waiting.

That's why editors apply pressure. These are the pressure tactics newspapers use on internship candidates—and how you can deal with them.

Early offers

Some papers will try to beat their competitors by making early offers. Sometimes, even large newspapers offer early. Almost every paper has called candidates too late to get them.

I once made an offer to a student who told me that she had an offer from another paper but that she had not accepted. When she told me that the offer had been made more than a month earlier and was still open, I became suspicious. I didn't think any editor would wait a month for a decision. The point of an early offer is to tie someone up, not to give that person a comfortable cushion. So, I called the editor at the other newspaper and asked whether the intern had, in fact, accepted. She had. The editor and the intern had agreed on a pay rate and a note had been posted in the other paper's newsroom announcing the hire. I called the candidate back and told her that she had accepted the offer, that the other paper was expecting her and that I would not do anything to tempt her to break her word. I also told her that I expected her to work in that other newsroom.

The earliest offer I've even seen? In August, 2004, the Portland *Oregonian* made an offer for the next year, ten months away. In 2005, I saw August offers coming out of Reuters and the *St. Petersburg Times*. The trend is growing.

Exploding offers

A sophomore I had interviewed at Northwestern University's Medill School of Journalism called in October to say that a paper had made her an offer with the stipulation that she accept it within forty-eight hours or lose it. I call an early offer with a short fuse and a threat an exploding offer.

I then knew that she would have an internship the next summer, in addition to one Medill would arrange for her during her junior year and, probably, internships after her junior and senior years. I knew she would go far, so I broke my usual practice of waiting for our December 1 deadline to make offers. I made my first offer of the year during that phone call and purposely set a roomy deadline. I gave her a week and encouraged her to consult with her family, friends, and profs. I told her I wanted her to go with us, but that I wanted her to feel comfortable and would not rush her. She turned down the other paper, went with ours and went on to work with the *Miami Herald,* the *Los Angeles Times,* and the *New York Times.*

No offer lasts forever, but an especially short decision window seems to go kaboom. Some newspapers set copy-editing offers to expire the day before they know that the Dow Jones Newspaper Fund will make offers to copy editing candidates. These offers are timed to eliminate the competition of a Newspaper Fund internship by setting a decision window that slams shut before Dow Jones picks are made. At the Dow Jones Newspaper Fund selection team, we often ask candidates whether they have already accepted something. If they have, we congratulate them and move on. Be concerned about a newspaper that, as it offers one opportunity, snatches another away. It is not acting in your best long-term interests and is hinting that the other offer would be better.

Dow Jones Newspaper Fund offers must be accepted the day they are made because they are part of a program that has a dozen people in New Jersey making more than a hundred offers over two days. I do not consider Dow Jones offers to be exploding offers because of that dynamic and because, when people apply, they are told when the offers will come and that the decision window will be very short. Dow Jones is not trying to beat other papers; it is just trying to get a big job done.

The finalists' pool

Be wary when a newspaper tells you that you are a finalist for an internship. Some newspapers tell a large number of applicants that they are all finalists. Of course, this implies that everyone is within a whisker of getting an internship and discourages them from accepting other offers. As it turns out, sometimes only a few finalists are chosen. The ploy strings good people along and keeps them off the market as the paper takes its time picking through the pool, one person at a time. If a newspaper tells you that you are a finalist, ask:

- How many finalists are there?
- How many positions are there?
- When will offers be made?
- Will offers be made all at once or in sequence?
- Has the newspaper made any offers yet?
- Will the newspaper be able to give me an answer if I receive a firm offer somewhere else?

Do not flatly turn down an offer because you are a finalist somewhere. Instead, call the paper that has you as a finalist, tell it you have an offer and ask for a decision. The paper likely will ask who has made the offer. You can tell, but it is wiser and more professional not to. Say, "I'm sorry, but don't think I can say at this point."

If a newspaper tells you after the selections have all been made that you were a finalist, this is not a pressure tactic. It is intended to be a compliment and a consolation. I do not tell people they were finalists. I think that hearing you were a finalist for something you did not get is about like missing the lottery by one number.

Threats

Some editors will darkly hint—or outright say—that you're making a big mistake to go with some paper other than their own. The implication, of course, is that you will be banned for life somehow if you don't take this internship. Don't believe it. If someone would banish you for accepting a good offer, you probably should not work for them, anyway. More realistically, if you are good enough to get the offer and you decline graciously, they'll probably want you later—when you're better—even more than they want you now.

One student applied for a summer internship and was told she could have it—if she quit her job as an editor at the school paper and began working part-time for the daily right away. The local paper had pulled students from her school paper before. She told the editor she felt she had to keep her commitment to the college paper and to staffers who worked for her. She wanted to serve her term. The editor crossly told her, "so much for your career." That's scary stuff when you're a college student. She stuck with the college paper. Her integrity helped her earn an internship at a newspaper that was five times larger than the original paper. The smaller paper persisted with an offer for part-time work during the following school year, but the threat had soured her.

Occasionally, candidates feel that an editor or newspaper will "blackball" them with other editors in the industry. One reporter felt that an editor implied that if she left a two-year internship program at his paper early to accept a job offer, he would use his power to block her chances of getting on at other newspapers. Although it felt scary to the reporter, it's nonsense. After all, she already had her next job.

People in the newspaper business are well connected, but the connections are loose. They know each other, but they do not control each other. Few editors have power beyond the immediate newspaper or newspaper company—although some companies contain dozens of newspapers. You will not damage your career by politely declining an offer. That kind of damage can only come from serious ethical, professional, or legal infractions.

Turning down offers

One of the toughest experiences of a new career is telling one newspaper no so that you can tell another one yes. Do it graciously and be brief. Do not say anything negative about the newspaper you're declining and say as little as possible about why you prefer the other. Reasons and rationalizations seldom make editors feel better.

Try not to give detailed reasons for your decision. They almost always sound like insults:

"I like your paper a lot, but the other one has a bigger reputation."

"They offered me more money."

"I'm just going with my instincts on this."

Try not to give any reasons that might eliminate you from future opportunities:

"Well, I decided to go to that paper because it's in an area where I'd like to live."

"I prefer cities."

Try something like this:

"Thanks so much for your offer. I was really quite flattered and grateful. This is difficult for me, but I am going to decline the offer. I was also offered a position at the *Mirror*, and I am going to accept that. I do like your paper and plan to stay in touch."

This answer contains no reasons, it compliments the paper you've rejected and it leaves the door open for future opportunities. Notice that it does not ask the editor to keep in touch. The editor, having lost a good intern, may not feel excited about that at the moment of rejection. But it informs the editor that the candidate will be making the effort to keep the connection alive. Do not make that promise if you have no desire to work at that paper in the future.

It is a bit nicer, but not necessary for you to tell editors that you have made a decision and are about to accept the other offer, rather than to tell them after it is a done deal. If you do this, under no circumstances can you tell them the name of the other paper. The paper you go with deserves the greater loyalty and you don't want them to hear about your choice from anyone other than you. Letting the also-rans know how things are developing makes them feel as though they have been kept in the loop and are part of the decision process. But it can open the door for them to pressure you one last time. The defensive strategy is to say, "Look, I have made my decision and am not going to change it. I just wanted to let you know what is going on."

While you should not tell editors about the papers you were considering while you were in your decision window, it is fine to tell them where you're going after you make your commitment. In fact, you should. They're going to find out anyway, and this will help them track you.

Handling late offers

What do you do when the offer you really wanted comes after you've already accepted another?

Once you accept an offer, stick with it. In journalism, where trust and integrity are so important, a person who breaks commitments soon gains a reputation—a bad one. So, don't back out, not even if you get a much better offer a month after your initial acceptance. Honorable editors will not ask people to break their commitments, and you should wonder about those who do. The newspaper universe is a small one. How small? This small:

I had come from Michigan to the University of North Carolina at Chapel Hill, where some of us were training Dow Jones Newspaper Fund interns. Four of us were at dinner when Newspaper Fund Executive Director Richard Holden showed me an e-mail on his handheld. The message had been sent to his account at the Newspaper Fund in Princeton, New Jersey, by an intern in San Francisco, She was pulling out of an internship in Myrtle Beach, South Carolina, at the last minute. "Hey," I said, "I know this person." I recalled our interview from a convention two years earlier in San Diego. My cell phone rang. Reggie Stuart, a recruiter based in Maryland, was calling to tell me that the newspaper in Myrtle Beach needed a new intern. One intern, a few people, six states. The world can be as small as that table.

Rarely, and for reasons that are a lot more serious than better offers, you may have to back out. For serious health or personal reasons when you really have no choice, this is understandable. But there are borderline cases. Here's one:

I had offered an internship in Detroit to a woman in Philadelphia who happened to be a single mother. She was excited to get the offer, because she thought she could arrange childcare for her daughter with a relative in Detroit. After she accepted the *Free Press* offer, she got an offer from another media company (not a newspaper) that would have kept her and her daughter at their home in Philly. She called me and explained. By, now, other good candidates I had been interested in were gone. We talked about her having the other company change its internship dates a little so that she could accept both offers and keep her pledge to work in Detroit. The other company would not budge. To make matters worse, I learned that the other company had known about the Detroit offer all along and had made its offer anyway, knowing that it was putting her in a difficult spot. When she found that the other company would not budge, she called, distraught, to tell me that she would keep her promise, but that she fervently wished the other company had been more flexible or, at least, speedier.

I said, "I'll tell you what. We are releasing you from your commitment. You do not have to keep your promise. You can stay in Philadelphia." It was as if a weight had been lifted from her shoulders. She could take the job with the inflexible company, keep her daughter in

Philadelphia and keep her reputation. I had to go find another intern, but felt we needed to do this for her and her child.

And that was a borderline call.

Since that time, in rare cases, I have advised people to ask editors to release them from their commitments. In each case, the editors agreed. Before the candidates asked to be released from commitments, though, we talked about what they would do if the editors said no. They agreed that, if they were to try this strategy, they needed to have a very good reason and they needed to abide by the editor's decision. In other words, they were prepared to go to the internship if the editor asked them to.

One student I had been tracking told me that, for the summer after her sophomore year, she had accepted an offer from a newspaper that was much smaller than what she had been hoping for. She simply panicked. A little while after she accepted that offer, a newspaper about four times the size of the first one offered her an internship.

What did she do?

She talked to her father, she talked with professors, but she already knew in her heart what to do. She kept her word.

"Really," I baited, "is that smart—to stick with the smaller paper?"

"It just seemed to be the right thing to do. You have to keep your word. Journalists go to jail to keep their commitments."

Bingo. That sign of integrity means more to me than the larger paper's name on her résumé would have meant.

Most of the time, you'll be in far better shape if you keep your word and stick with the newspaper that wanted you first and most. They had confidence in you; repay that with commitment. The only person sorrier than the one who misses a shot at the second newspaper is the one who breaks an agreement with the first newspaper and is disappointed.

Coping with rejection

We're going to handle rejection in two ways: seriously and with a sense of humor.

Seriously, it is no fun getting rejected. It's happened to me, it's happened to you and it's happened to everyone we know. It feels lousy. The most successful people you know have drunk from that bitter cup, even though it may seem that they never missed out on anything in their lives. The person who never got rejected is the person who never really reached. You have to defeat the feeling of being defeated. If you let rejection smack you down for more than a day, you won't succeed. Rejection is the byproduct of ambition.

We know we need to deal with rejection, to get past it and, ideally to learn from it. Rejection has a lot more to teach us than success does, but few of us want to go to that school.

Getting rejected has a strange way of pushing us toward success. No one who is hot off a turndown wants to hear a cheery "everything happens for a reason" or "when one door closes, another opens." These aphorisms are true only for the people who keep trying. The person who finds a good opportunity after the first one vaporized made that second opportunity happen by refusing to give up.

One who won: *The State News* at Michigan State University is one of the largest student newspapers in the country. It is so competitive that students have to go through a portfolio review and a panel interview just to intern. And this is a *student* paper. Many campus papers would love to see someone walk in the door, but this one regularly shuts it. One student who was rejected by the student paper can laugh today because, in the same year she was turned down by her fellow students, she was chosen for an internship at the *Detroit Free Press*. The ones who voted her out were not chosen at the *Free Press*. That rejected student went on to become a White House correspondent for the Associated Press. And how does she get along today with some of the people who worked for that student paper? They're friends. And maybe it's her resilience that helped her get through that heart-breaking rejection and to where she is today.

Keeping your sense of humor helps you get past the pain—which you have to do—and gets you back on track. Getting mired in rejection hurts one person—you—not the people who rejected you, or anyone else.

Too many times, rejection comes in the form of the silent treatment:

- One person who had applied to me by e-mail, and whom I rejected in an e-mail, wrote back to say thanks for letting her know. I wrote back that things must be pretty tough, when even rejections generate thank-you's. She replied that many editors don't even take the time to say no. She was happy just to get an answer.

- Once, the managing editor at a mid-sized paper called and asked if I could quickly give him the name of a good internship candidate. He had just found out that he had an internship to fill and that he had to make a decision quickly. I asked whether he had received any good applications at his own paper. He said he had, but that he didn't have time to go through them and that he thought I could just give him a name quickly. I did and the intern did a great job for them. That was terribly unfair to the people who had applied there, but the net result—one internship filled—was the same as if he had applied himself. It was, though, ineffective that year to apply to his newspaper, as applications didn't get read, and slightly better to apply to mine because I wound up with an unexpected opportunity somewhere else.
- I called an editor at another mid-size paper and asked about a student who had applied there and hadn't hear back. "Just a minute," he said as he dove under his desk to rifle through the box of mail under there. "Ah, here it is! I'm the city editor and the internship coordinator and I really don't have time to answer all of these."
- A major metro's recruiter, now retired, got a call from an internship applicant who asked where her application stood. The recruiter told the candidate that she would get a call if she landed an internship—but not if she didn't.

These are funny stories—unless they've happened to you. But this is the reality. Many rejections are really just you-figure-it-out silences.

Newspapers must have enough staffing and their acts together to send word on internship decisions. These can be worse than no answers at all.

Rejection letters

Don't you hate it when the person writing the letter tells the person being rejected how tough the process is? They should get such a letter to understand what tough feels like. And those letters that try to make you fell better by saying that six hundred other people were also rejected? Misery may love company, but it does not like being part of a whole country.

From time to time, a newspaper will send out postcard rejections.

John Kupetz was an instructor at Northwestern University's Medill School of Journalism and the guru of its career services office. He said newspapers forget that a lot of internship candidates still live in dorms, so a rejection postcard that goes into the mailroom at their dorm tells the whole dorm that they failed.

As someone who sends out rejections—in batches—I didn't really know what it is like on the receiving end—until my son started applying in his field. It's damn discouraging. He would read and reread each letter, trying to tease the clues out of them. Why was he rejected? He found a lot of things in those letters—typos, for one. And ridiculous statements, too. Remember that these are form letters. They do not contain any specific information that can help you tune up for the next round of applications.

Guest: The rejection letter of all rejection letters

By JOHN FRANK
Staff Writer
The Potomac News

Even in dismal job markets, applicants flood the market with their applications for internships.

I applied for internships at more than fifteen newspapers, which is merely half the number sent out by most of my colleagues at the school newspaper.

Yet, sending more applications usually doesn't work. The only thing it guarantees is more rejection letters.

Once you get one letter you feel like you've gotten them all. After a while they start to sound alike because they are, after all, form letters. And you have to admit, some of the letters are amusing.

So I didn't dwell on my bad fortune last year. And neither should you.

Combining a dozen of the letters that flooded my mailbox last winter, I have prepared "The Rejection Letter of All Rejection Letters."

So even if it seems like it can't get worse, just be glad you didn't get this rejection letter:

Dear internship candidate: (1)

Thank you for your inquiry. (2) And for the time and work you spent putting together your application. The intern review committee has spent many hours reading these applications, and we have found something fresh and interesting in each of them. (3)

I want to compliment you on putting together a strong application and wish you well as you take the next step in your development as a journalist. (4)

Your application was among nearly four hundred we received, and we are honored that you would consider our paper as a place where you would want to work. (5)

One of the blessings of hearing from so many well-qualified applicants is knowing that we'll have a strong group this year. One of the disappointments, however, is realizing that we don't have enough internship slots to go around for everyone. (4)

While I am happy to have considered you, I regret to say that you have not been selected for an internship this summer. (6) Unfortunately, you were not one of the final ten. (7)

We use a variety of criteria to select our interns, including previous internship experience and work samples. (8)

Please do not be discouraged; there is always tough competition for internships, and not every good applicant will succeed in a particular year. (3) Numbers alone forced us to turn down many applicants with superior talent. (9)

We also regret that the number of applications has made it impossible for use to send you a more personal letter. Please be assured, however, that your application was carefully read and evaluated. (9)

We are confident that you'll find other opportunities. Keep up the good work and best of luck in the coming year and beyond. (5)

John Frank is a staff writer at The St. Petersburg Times (which contributed part of this rejection letter). While attending the University of North Carolina, he suffered through major internship rejection before taking an unpaid gig at The Charlotte Observer. After graduating in 2004, he interned at The (Raleigh, North Carolina) News and Observer and then completed a political reporting fellowship at the Houston Chronicle's Washington Bureau. He worked as a statehouse reporter for The (Charleston, South Carolina) Post and Courier before he was hired by the Times in 2006.

Gaining summer journalism experience at a daily newspaper of any size will prove invaluable as you launch your search for a professional position upon graduation. (1)

The Web site for the American Society of Newspaper Editors features a list of smaller newspapers and there is still time for you to land an internship if you haven't done so already! (10)

This is a challenging and exciting time to be in the profession, and it's great to know there are so many bright young journalists getting ready to join in. (3)

Although you were not chosen this year, you are invited to apply again if you are enrolled for the next school year. (11) We will keep your application on file, but please keep us posted as your studies and career progress. Also, feel free to send us updated work samples. (7)

Thank you again for your interest, (12)

1. *The Denver Post*
2. *The* (South Florida) *Sun-Sentinel*
3. *The Austin American-Statesman*
4. *The Oregonian*
5. *The Boston Globe*
6. *The St. Petersburg Times*
7. *The Raleigh News & Observer*
8. *The Los Angeles Times*
9. *The Washington Post*
10. *The Atlanta Journal-Constitution*
11. *The* (New Orleans) *Times-Picayune*
12. *USA TODAY* ✺

Creative uses of rejection letters

People who do mass internship applications will get more rejection letters than at any other time in their lives. It is not an encouraging way to start a career. Fortunately, there are some very therapeutic ways to use those letters. One person we know who is now an editor framed a rejection letter, along with a clipping that later announced the closing of the paper. That seems mean. But, consider his mood. Other ideas:

• Some college-town bars give out a free drink for every "bullet" or "ding"—rejection letter. Are there any in your town?
• Decoupage your wastebasket with rejection letters.

- Line your bird's cage with them. Which paper will Polly pick?
- Make them into paper airplanes and throw them out the window. Although you may be tempted, do not set them on fire.
- Search the letters for lines that can be excerpted into testimonials. "We heard from many people who have excellent experience and clips" can boil down to "excellent experience and clips." Put the excerpts on your reference page—and attribute them to the newspapers that wrote them.
- Search the letter for typos. Circle them and mail the letters back to the editors. Cut your name off first.
- If it is a generic form letter addressed to "candidate," write a thank-you to the person who sent it. Sign your letter "candidate."
- Memorize the names of people who write you rejection letters so that you can run into them someday—while driving.
- With your friends, organize a game of rejection letter lotto. Give yourself points for each of the problems you find in your rejection letters:

   Name spelled wrong: five points.
   Wrong gender: ten points.
   No name at all: three points.
   Additional typos: one point each

6

Making the Most of Your Internship

OK, you've landed a newspaper internship. Hooray! Take a bow!

Now, you're just a little nervous about things. How will you do? Where will you live? How will people treat you? As a peer or like a kid? Will you get the clips you want? Will you do something really stoopid?

Hey, don't stress! Relax!

That's Tip No. 1 for a successful internship: Relax.

We newspaper editors are extremely wise (and humble), and would never have chosen you if you couldn't hack it. We have confidence in you; have confidence in yourself.

Feeling more relaxed? Good. Keep reading.

Preparation

I wasn't in the elevator when this happened, so I'm giving this to you secondhand from someone who was there. Some *New York Times* interns got into the elevator at the newspaper and a nice man got in with them. Introductions began.

"Hi, I'm so-and-so and I'm interning here. Who are you?"

"I'm Arthur Sulzberger."

"Oh, and what do you do here?"

"I'm the publisher."

"Oh ... "

Why DO elevators move so slowly when you really, really need to get out of them?

Do not walk into your newspaper with so much ignorance that you can bring that kind of embarrassment down on yourself.

I was working with a group of Dow Jones Newspaper Fund interns in their pre-internship training camp and asked them who the editors of their newspapers were. Few knew. But all had Internet access and found out within minutes.

In the time between when you accept the offer and when you arrive, become an avid student of the newspaper. Do your reporting. Read the paper regularly—online and on paper. Request a copy of the stylebook and learn it. Get maps of the city. Check newspaper stories against those maps to see where things happen. If you can, visit the city and the newspaper, or arrive a few days early to look around.

Countdown to a successful internship

Here is a checklist for the weeks leading up to your internship.

10. Nail down the details: When will you report, where and to whom?
9. Find a place to live.
8. Arrange transportation for your new job, both how you will get to the city and how you will get around it.
7. Start reading the newspaper thoroughly and continue this habit through your internship and your career. Read the newspaper on paper and online, as each version is unique and one may not include everything that is in the other.
6. Learn the policies. Ask for a copy of the newspaper's stylebook and whether there is a procedures or orientation handbook. Get and learn the ethics policy. Ask whether this information is posted on the newspaper's Intranet and whether you may have a guest password that will let you in there until the day when you become a staff member.

JobsPage in My Pocket

Basic facts to know before you hit town.

Publisher:
Editor:
Other editors in the masthead:
Editor of your section:
Corporate owner or if it's independent:
Properties owned by the same company:
Daily circulation:
Major competitors:
Evening or morning delivery:
When the paper was founded:
You can learn all of this on the Web and with a copy of the newspaper.

---

5. Read outside sources about the community. What books have been written about that community? Do the editors have any suggestions? (They will be impressed and you will have an icebreaker if you read a book they recommend.) Is there another newspaper in town? An alternative newspaper? A city magazine? What can you get from the local chamber of commerce? Study road and bus maps to get familiar with the layout of the town, its roads, rivers, and other major features.

4. Visit the community. Try to get there early enough to do some driving around or use the bus system. Ask strangers about the community and the newspaper.

3. Before you start work, take a dry run to make sure you know how to get there. Locate the newspaper and, if you'll be driving, the parking.

2. Get familiar with the names of people you're likely to meet. Can you find a staff roster online? Will the paper send you one? Whom have you already talked to? Start a list. What names do you see in the masthead and atop section fronts? What bylines and photo credits can you associate with recent work in the newspaper? You may be about to meet an overwhelming number of people, and a little anticipation may help the day go better. It will help you, too, if you can say to someone, "Yes, I chuckled when I read your column on potholes in yesterday's paper."

1. Show up early on your first day with a notebook, your Social Security card (not just the number), driver's license, proof of auto insurance and citizenship.

Focus

As an intern, you have a lot going on. You may be a student as well as someone who is expected to do a professional job.

As college has growing numbers of options for study and travel, and as journalism conventions and training opportunities are multiplying, new journalists find more and more reasons to interrupt their internships.

One intern asked if he could leave his internship for a week to attend a prestigious, invitation-only seminar. I agreed.

Then, he asked whether he could leave for a few days to attend a journalism convention. I hesitated, but agreed.

When he asked for a third interruption, I said no.

He went over my head—all the way to corporate—to complain that I wasn't being flexible. The bosses said I was doing the right thing. By the end of his internship, he agreed. He said that the time away distracted him and hurt his internship, which was really the most important part of his summer. The other options were just add-ons. Nice, but not as important.

An intern was selected for a prestigious internship and went into its accompanying training program with plans to spend part of his time training for the internship and part of his time on schoolwork. His instructor rightfully concluded that the intern wasn't focused or serious enough to do his best work. The intern was sent home from the training program and lost a highly coveted and highly paid internship.

Before coming to the *Free Press,* an intern asked whether he could take a summer course during his internship. "What will happen if the summer's big story breaks and you have to leave for a 7 p.m. class? What will happen if you have the chance to work on a big news day, but need to be in class?" He chose to focus on his internship, instead, had a great time and learned a lot.

Now, newspapers need to accommodate the balanced lives that people want to live. But balance implies equal weight on both sides of the scale. Family is important, so is career and so is commitment. If you promise to take an internship, make it your top work-related priority while you're there. Family concerns may intervene, and most editors will help you with those, but interruptions for a second job or a summertime course send the wrong signal. Let's make one exception: If you are working an unpaid internship, you may have to make a higher commitment to another job, and you may have to let that get in the way of journalistic opportunity.

Goals

If you're planning to go nowhere, that's exactly where you'll wind up.

Go into your internship with a map in one hand, a compass in the other and an itinerary in the—oh, never mind.

Set goals.

Goals teach you to accomplish objectives and give your career momentum and direction. Without goals, how are we to know whether we have accomplished anything?

Set just a few goals. Twenty is unrealistic. Ten, too.

Set a few goals that will require you to stretch, that are important to where you want to take your career and that are more or less in your control.

Have reasonable expectations. A lot of interns expect to earn thirty bylines. Or forty. Or fifty. Others pledge to commit no errors. Or to turn the internship into a job. But internships are not measured in bylines or job offers or absolute perfection. Here's a more reasonable expectation: Plan and work to improve as a journalist. Learning from practice and experience is the real purpose of an internship, so put your goals there. You're not being realistic and you're missing a key point if you build your goals around earning a certain number of bylines or a job in a newsroom where, perhaps, you have never set foot. Set learning goals, and measure your experience by demonstrating new skills. Be open. Success may come in ways you did not expect.

These can be useful goals, depending on what you have already done and the type of job you are working toward:

"I will cover a trial."

"I will use the Freedom of Information Act to report a story."

"I will improve my leads to the point where two-thirds of them are used essentially as I wrote them."

"I will become better at pitching my own story ideas and will pitch at least one story every week."

"I will try to work with a team of reporters on a big story so that I can see how they work together."

"I will go totally digital with my photography."

"I will write something every day."

JobsPage in My Pocket

My goals for this internship:

1.
2.
3.
4.
5.
6.

"I will develop a system that helps my accuracy. My goal it to have no errors in the paper, and none that editors have to catch."

These goals are more qualitative or experiential than quantitative and require you to acquire and apply new skills. Are they totally within your control? Not all of them. The photo director may not want to have everything shot in a digital format. But by discussing goals with your editor, the two of you can craft achievable goals. And when you enlist your editor as a partner, you are working on those goals together. This lends much more meaning to an internship than setting a production number that is, in many ways, uninformed.

Professional relationships

One of the best missed opportunities for many interns is the chance to find a good editor or mentor. Some people drift into the internship, work hard and then disappear. They don't seem to understand what internships are for. They don't pick the brains around them, they develop no sustainable relationships and then they drift away.

Smart interns find mentors, cultivate editors to be references, and stay in touch.

Internships are not just summer-help programs. Internships are a way for employers to identify and cultivate employees for their company or other companies in the industry. Interns who understand this stay in the loop.

Mentors are a chief benefit of an internship. You'll need mentors for several different kinds of advice, but all will be safe, supportive people who can help you understand the business and get better at it. A mentor can be your editor, your editor's editor, or a non-supervisor who shows interest in you and your work.

Some papers will assign mentors or partners to the people they hire. Some don't. In either case, getting a good mentor is your responsibility. It is certainly not the mentor's responsibility to sign up. And you cannot leave it to the newspaper to guess about who will be a good match. Mentoring relationships can spring up informally. Or, you can quite deliberately ask someone whose work and style you respect, "Would you be my mentor?" For some of us, this is a great compliment.

Personal relationships

When you get hired as an intern, you are as a professional, but you come aboard as a person, too. The distinction between the professional you and the personal you is not always clear. The line gets blurred, quite naturally, when you make friends at work. This is a good and healthy thing and internships often lead to lifelong friendships.

When you become intimate with co-workers, though, you blur the line so badly that your personal actions can make people doubt your judgment—even in professional matters. When people find out—and they do, this IS a newspaper, after all—that an intern has started an intimate relationship with another intern or a permanent staffer, some will wonder whether the intern has stars in the eyes or rocks in the head. You could look foolish, naïve, or inappropriate.

I'm sure you would consider your physical, emotional, and mental well-being before you began any intimate relationship.

Know that when you become intimate with a co-worker, whether during this internship or in a later job, you also have to weigh whether you are jeopardizing everything you've done to have a healthy career.

Again, feel free to form long-term, meaningful relationships, but watch out for flings that could hurt you.

Ethics

The surest way to torpedo your career and the reputations of the people around you is to violate the basic ethics of journalism. The stakes

---

JobsPage in My Pocket

Stopping harassment

Most professional workplaces have strong anti-harassment policies. If you are getting attention from someone who makes you feel uncomfortable, this is the first step.

Say to the harasser: "I need you to stop (the behavior) because it makes me feel uncomfortable. If you don't stop it, I will report you to one of our supervisors." If this doesn't works, go to a manager in the newsroom or human resources. Speaking to a co-worker may help you feel better, but is not likely to bring any relief.

are high. We have seen editors at the *New York Times* and *USA TODAY* lose their jobs because staff members acted unethically. We have seen a *Los Angeles Times* photographer in Iraq fired on the spot for submitting an image he had doctored. Don't come back; your job is over. And he knew it.

If top editors must pay with their jobs for unethical behavior committed on their watches, what does this say about interns? You could lose your job, too, and live in infamy on the Internet.

Know this: While people who behaved unethically used to got second chances, those days seem to be over. One strike and you're out. Too many people who seemed to have had momentary lapses did it again. No newspaper feels safe taking a chance with someone who has been unethical, even once.

Worse than the damage you to do your career is the harm this does to all the earnest, honest, hard-working people in the industry who will be doubted because another journalist took a shortcut. Don't do it.

The basic ethics of journalism are:

- Tell the truth
- Be accurate
- Stay independent

People lie and steal when their byline says that the material is theirs, but they got it from someone else.

People lie when they claim that fiction really happened.

People lose their independence when they accept special treatment for doing their jobs.

If your newspaper does not send you an ethics policy, ask for it. Some do not have them because attorneys have advised the newspaper it is better not to have policies that it can be flogged with in court. In other newsrooms, unions have insisted there can be no code until it is negotiated into the contract. If your newspaper does not have an ethics policy, think hard about your own ethical principles so you will have a compass to follow when you are tested.

One reporter had such a strict personal policy against accepting anything for her work that she declined journalism awards and once sent back an empty ostrich eggshell the local zoo had given her as thanks for an article she had written. Her personal ethics code was to accept nothing, period.

These are the ways that people violate journalistic ethics.

Plagiarism

If it was not your idea, don't act as though it was. No one else's words should find their way into your articles, except as direct quotes.

Artists can plagiarize ideas, too, by closely mimicking another artist's work.

If you are writing but think that the words coming together in front of you may be words you read or heard somewhere else, take another tack.

Fabrication

Never invent anything for the newspaper. If you didn't see it happen or hear it said, don't pretend you did. You cannot use composite people or recreate scenes that you did not see.

Independence

The best journalism happens because it is of importance and interest to our community. If, because others do favors for us, we start to do our jobs differently, the community is badly served. We cannot accept favors or special privileges for being journalists. We have to avoid situations that might put us in that position—or even make it look that way to people.

Avoiding mistakes

Making mistakes can be just as damaging to the newspaper and to you as unethical behavior is. This raises care and accuracy to the same level of importance as honesty.

An editor who was preparing to speak to college professors at the American Press Institute asked editors on a listserv for the No. 1 thing she could tell the professors that students needed to know before walking into the newsroom

I was surprised.

The Edge ⎯⎯⎯⎯⎯⎯⎯⎯⎯⎯⎯⎯⎯⎯⎯⎯⎯⎯⎯⎯⎯⎯⎯⎯⎯⎯⎯⎯⎯⎯⎯

The American Society of Newspaper Editors, the largest organization of editors in the country, has posted dozens of ethics codes. Read a couple. They will push you to think about your personal code. http://www.asne.org/ideas/codes/codes.htm

They told her the students need to work harder at being accurate. That's all: simple accuracy.

But accuracy is not so simple. In the hurry to meet daily deadlines, relying on sources that don't always get things right, and being human, we make mistakes.

A professor at the University of Maryland based an article for the American Journalism Review on the observations of his students. One had said: "Being 99 percent accurate will get you fired."

Use the strategies that veterans use to earn reputations for being rock-solid accurate:

- Always, always edit yourself before you let your article go. That means giving yourself an earlier deadline than the editor does. If you have to turn it in at 4 p.m., plan to be done writing at 3:30 p.m. and self-edit. Keep checking your story after you've turned it in and speak up if you've missed something. Pay special attention to facts—all facts. Be especially careful with the facts that are our most common source of trouble: names, numbers, and historical dates—including history as recent as last week.
- Never guess. Never assume. Look it up.
- Never take the lazy attitude that your editor or the copy desk will "catch it." You'll be the one to catch it if your sloppiness gives your editor a nervous condition.
- Some of the most accurate writers use this technique: After they have written their stories, they print them out and then literally go over them with a pencil, circling and verifying every fact.
- Other reporters like to read their stories over again in a column that is narrower than full-screen width. They say they spot things when the lines are not so wide.
- Do not use a spelling checker as a crutch.
- When you get the names of people you interview, have them write their names in your notebook. When you ask for their age, get the date and year of birth. Some people get their own ages wrong but seldom bobble their birth year. And a person who is thirty-five on one day can be thirty-six the next—it all depends on the birthday. If your notes have the date of birth, you can avoid a birthday surprise that puts an inaccurate age in the newspaper.
- If you take facts over the phone, read back to verify that what you think you heard is what the sources think they said.

- Check facts, even when they come from reliable sources. At the *Detroit Free Press,* the people who compile calendars handle enormous streams of information. One says that almost every press release has a mistake in it, so she makes a lot of calls to double-check. That is scary.
- Verify every phone number by calling the number you have typed on the computer, not by calling the number that is in your notes. If you type it wrong and call from your notes, you won't catch it.
- Check every Web address, again, from the story as it appears on your screen.

Recovering from mistakes

Despite every precaution, you will make mistakes.

You make them and so do i. (oops)

The issue is not just whether we make mistakes, it's what we do after we make them.

The root of the appropriate response lies in understanding what mistakes do. Mistakes damage your newspaper's credibility, your own credibility and the credibility of the people who work with you and in journalism generally.

If readers cannot trust us to get things right, we have nothing. Good journalists fiercely maintain, protect and, when necessary, try to restore that credibility. Here are the five steps to follow when you do the inevitable:

Admit responsibility. Do not point fingers at others who may have participated in the mistake or let it get through. Anyone who has worked at a newspaper for more than a week should know that it is a

---

I have a spelling checker
it came with my PC
It plainly marks for my revue,
Mistake I cannot sea.
I've run this poem threw it,
I'm sure your please too no.
It's letter perfect in it's weigh,
My checker tolled me sew.
—*Author Unknown*

rare mistake that belongs to just one person. Your editors know this, too. Admitting responsibility is far better than having responsibility pinned on you as you try to shift blame.

Show remorse. Not sack cloth and ashes, but genuine concern for the trouble and the misunderstanding the mistake has caused readers. Apologies to sources and editors may be appropriate.

Make things right. You can't get the mistake back once it's been published, but you should offer to write the correction. If the newspaper has a third party writing the corrections—a good policy—offer to help.

Explain. Don't point fingers. The last thing we want to see from someone who has just been involved in a mistake is that they accuse others. So, don't make excuses when you explain. If you went too fast, were careless or failed to check the best sources, say so. Some newspapers want to see this in writing. Anticipate that and write your explanation even before someone asks for it. Can these be used against you at appraisal time? Yes. But there will be no need for that if you make very few mistakes, and invoking your Fifth Amendment rights won't save you, anyway. After all, the evidence of the mistake—without your explanation—has been published and delivered all around town.

Learn and move on. Analyze how the mistake occurred and change your work habits to make sure it won't happen again. Then move on. Don't let remorse paralyze you. You're not the first journalist to make a mistake and you won't be the last. You won't really get over this mistake until you're confident that you're producing error-free journalism again. Get to it.

Feedback and criticism

Everyone likes feedback. Especially if it is nice. Feedback that is not music to our ears is criticism. When it is constructive, criticism helps us grow faster than warm and fuzzy feedback.

You should learn to tolerate, then appreciate and seek out criticism.

The first step is to use it well. Constructive criticism, which can

---

" Mistakes are a fact of life. It's the response to the error that counts. **"**

—*Nikki Giovanni, poet*

come at the editing stage or after something is published, is not criticism of you. It is criticism of a story, decision, image, or something else you made or did. The first step is to detach yourself from your work—not easy—and look at it with the same outsider's eye as the person who criticized it. It is not a You vs. Them situation, so don't get defensive. That's easy to say, but hard to do. We find that all kind of newspaper people—including some of the nation's high-ranking editors—are very defensive. On the other hand, we find that some of the newest are wonderfully adept at separating themselves from their work and hearing criticism without feeling as though someone has just called them a horrible person.

Using criticism to improve means understanding how you could have taken a different action or made a different decision to come out with a better result—and how you can do that the next time. That's learning.

Many journalists—not just interns—wish their editors were harder on them. They want to be challenged to be good, better, best. Harried editors, or those who are afraid of hurting feelings, do not push enough.

In those cases, push your editor to push you.

Guest: The three Ps (or great expectations)

By GEORGE REDE
Director of Recruiting and Training
The Oregonian

Congratulations! You've just landed the internship or entry-level job you were hoping for. All the time and effort you put into your application materials and preparing for your interviews paid off. Now it's time to produce.

You may be feeling confident or nervous, or both, as you walk in the door, eager to show that the editor who hired you made a good decision. Knowing what the boss expects may help chase the butterflies and help you focus on qualities that will make you a valuable employee and trusted colleague, now and in the future.

Let's begin with two assumptions. One, talent and potential got you in the door, so we know you have a set of skills to build upon. Two, any list of desirable qualities is subjective, so don't take mine as definitive. (See following sidebar.)

After nearly three decades in journalism as a reporter, editor, and recruiter, I've developed a short list of qualities I keep in mind when talking to prospects, no matter if they are reporters, photographers, or copy editors. Let's call them The Three Ps.

Passion. It all begins here. Anyone can call himself a journalist, but an abiding love of the craft and respect for its role in society is what drives people to succeed. Too often, I hear people say, "I've always liked to write," or "I enjoy meeting people," without getting to the substance of why. Ours is the business of telling true stories, of holding people and institutions accountable, of making connections that aren't always easy to see. If you're invigorated by the diversity of people and places in your community, if you relish explaining how and why things happen (or don't), if you take pride in illuminating issues and ideas, there's a good chance you've got the natural curiosity and work ethic that together define passion.

Persistence. It continues here. To do journalism well inevitably means long or irregular hours. News often breaks late in the day, on holidays and weekends. And many sources can be hard to contact or reluctant to talk. Pitching in to cover the story of the day will help get you noticed as a team player. But over time, you also want to be known as someone who's resourceful, reliable and fair in getting a story. It takes a blend of tenacity and tact, of building trust and thinking on your feet. It means pushing beyond pat answers, challenging conventional wisdom and asking the uncomfortable question. Doing all of this with a strong ethical compass and a healthy respect for sources and readers will help you establish a reputation for integrity. Never giving up, always seeking a better way. That's persistence.

George Rede is director of recruiting and training at The Oregonian in Portland, Oregon. He coordinates newsroom hiring and manages the paper's internship and in-house training programs.

Precision. It underlies everything. Getting it right is what it's all about. Editors demand it. Readers deserve it. And you should always strive for it, knowing that our (and your) credibility is on the line every day, on every page.

Accuracy matters in every detail and aspect of what we do. It starts with the obvious—verifying names, ages, dates, and times; attributing information fully and fairly; doing the math to corroborate numbers and statistics. But there's more. Does the headline capture the essence and tone of the story? Does the caption accurately describe the action and explain the context of the picture?

Does the quote or paraphrase fairly represent the speaker's point of view? How do you know this? How do you know that? Passion and persistence will take you only so far. Let your work show that you bring care and commitment to getting the story right—precisely right.

Good luck in your new job and welcome to a wonderful profession.

P.S: Lighten up! Humility and humor go a long way.

What qualities are we looking for?

Everyone looks for talent when hiring young journalists. But what are the qualities that newspaper editors and recruiters look for when sizing up a prospect?

Editors came together at a conference at Poynter to consider that question in the context of recruiting and grooming the best and brightest. Prompted by Poynter's Gregory Favre, each person in the room, including a couple of observers, offered one quality.

Assuming talent as a given, here's what the group of executive editors, assistant managing editors, city editors and training editors came up with:

Character
Curiosity
Analytical skills
Passion (for journalism and their work)
Attitude of continuing learning (a desire to always get better)
Critical and conceptual thinking
Respect for readers
Humility

Creative attitude (a willingness to stretch themselves)
Good "fit" (someone who will be a good colleague)
Understanding of the role of journalism in democracy
Desire to do excellent work
Self-awareness (knowing their strengths and weaknesses)
Ability to reflect
Intelligence and intellectual vigor
Initiative
Potential for growth
Resilience and persistence
Diversity
Sense of humor
Collegiality
Commitment
Integrity and a keen sense of ethics
Care for local news

No one expects to find one individual with all these qualities, but we are looking for people who have enough of these qualities to justify not just their hiring but the additional investment of training to help them become the leaders in tomorrow's newsrooms. ✳

Housing

Few editors are as concerned about where interns will stay as the interns are. That just makes sense. One reason is self-interest. The other is that, while the intern has no idea where he or she will stay, the editors know that all of last year's interns stayed somewhere and things will work out. So, the help you get will not come as rapidly or as extensively as you might like. In the worst cases, there is no help. But you will find a place to live, whether your internship is in Alabama or Alaska.

There are horror stories. One person who is now an editor stayed on the back of her editor's property in a "modernized chicken coop." An intern at a Florida newspaper found a trailer home that had been previously occupied by a man, his dog, and his dog's fleas. Man and dog had moved out. Fleas stayed. That reporter bore fleabite scars for years. When she told her editors of her awful living conditions, they laughed. They told her she was better off than a previous intern, who had lived in his car.

It shouldn't be this way for you. The more comfortable you are with where you live, the better you'll work. The smart editors know this and will help you.

Here's how to avoid roosting with chickens or bedding down with fleas.

Begin with the editors who hired you. Ask:

- Do you have information about summer housing?
- Can you post a note to the staff asking whether anyone has a spare room?
- How can I reach last year's interns to ask where they stayed?
- How can I reach this year's interns to find a roommate and share housing information?

On your own:

Check the newspaper's classified ads for places with monthly leases. Check other papers, too. Try Craigslist.

Call the housing departments at local colleges and universities

Look for Web sites that list short-term leases in the area.

As you look, keep these things in mind:

If you'll have no car, look for places close to the newspaper, of course, but also look for places on major bus lines running near the newspaper. Most editors are clueless about public transportation. They all own cars, and the only way they catch a bus is if they jaywalk. They typically do not know the bus lines, how frequently the buses run or even how much the fare is. In fact, unless you are used to taking the bus yourself, this may seem unfamiliar to you, too. Relax. If you're any kind of journalist, you can learn the bus system. Ask to talk to someone at the newspaper who is a bus rider, or visit the transit system's Web site and get some maps. Remember: Summer is the best time for bus riding in most places, as the days are longer and the temperatures kinder.

Consider having a roommate. If you want to be alone, you'll pay for the privilege. We're talking ten or twelve weeks here with a person whose schedule may or may not line up with yours. Unless you're independently wealthy, at least talk to other interns to see whether you think you'd be compatible. Do not be so tight that you book yourself into a hold that will be so unpleasant it drags down your work.

It can be a great benefit to stay with a staffer. This can give you safe, secure housing, it's usually cheaper and you may find a mentor. However, some people who are charming in the newsroom are tyrannical on their own turf. Ask about house rules. Better yet, ask someone who has stayed with them before. Yes, ask for a reference. And don't be bothered if they want one for you.

It is fairly standard for apartment managers to ask you to get written confirmation from the paper that verifies your employment and rate of pay. Once you find a place, ask someone at the newspaper to tell you what the area is like. Before I was coordinating *Free Press* internships, I spent one summer as business editor. When the intern for our department arrived for work, I asked her where she lived. She named a scary neighborhood where she had found a cheap apartment. I gulped and asked her how she liked it. She said her apartment was fine, but she had noticed inside a fast-food restaurant nearby that someone had shot the doorknob off the bathroom door. We helped her find a new place.

Transportation

Your big concern is getting the internship, not getting to it. Do not put the cart before the horse. If you get hung up on not knowing how you'll get to a place before you try to find the internship, you'll be putting false barriers in your way. Think this way: If you can land the internship, you can damn sure get to it. There are buses. There are trains. Your friends need a road trip. One Michigan student flew to the California city where she was interning, bought a twenty-year-old used car, drove it for the summer and then sold it at the end. That helped her get a great internship, increased her confidence, and showed she is resourceful.

The Edge ————————————————————————

Living costs

When you move from a campus to a new city, a lot of living costs that were hidden or included show up as bills. Ask what your paycheck would be after taxes and find out whether there is a city income tax for residents. Ask landlords about utilities, cable, Internet access, and parking fees. Do they require a damage deposit plus a month of rent in advance?

Getting to an internship will not be a problem for those with initiative. Getting around during the internship can be an issue for anyone. If you are going to have a big problem on your internship that is not about journalism, it likely will have four wheels and a windshield. We have had interns who did not know how to drive, whose licenses were lost or suspended, who totaled company cars, who had their own cars stolen, who had to lease cars, who secretly amassed piles of parking tickets and one who crashed into the publisher's car. I have co-signed for interns to rent cars, taught them how to parallel park, and shown them how to change flat tires. All survived. Even the one who hit the publisher's car.

Find out whether you must have a car to do the job. Copy editors, artists, and designers need to get to the office, but they seldom need to go out. Reporters and photographers will be frustrated and miss good stories if the only thing they can ride is a desk. Not having a license or a car in a job where you really need one is like not having a telephone or a computer. These are the tools you need to do the job.

The interns had just started work and an exasperated editor on the metro desk called me.

"Joe, do you know that you hired another intern who can't drive?"

"Really? But she speaks three languages . . ."

In Detroit, the most important lingua is moto lingua. Parlez vous vroom-vroom?

This particular intern spent part of her summer learning to drive. She found it was as useful to a reporter as either Spanish or Japanese. We were so happy when our oldest intern got her license that we gave her a cake decorated with a little car. This made the youngest intern gripe, "She gets her license and she gets a cake; when I got my license, all I got was a lecture."

So, get a driver's license. I don't care if you grew up in Brooklyn, where the only people who drive are cabbies and crazies. In most of the country, we drive.

In a few cities—very few—public transportation will be all you need. And at a few newspapers, there is a pool of cars for people going out to write about or photograph stories. In those cases, find out whether it is practical to arrive without a car. Some newspapers that provide cars for work are in areas where you need a car to get to the housing—and they do not let interns borrow cars overnight. Otherwise, do what you can to beg, borrow—but do not steal—a car.

If you cannot get a loaner or buy a clunker, consider a rental, But do some checking. The big companies require renters to be of a certain age (twenty-five) and to have a credit card (not a debit card). So, have a credit card in your own name, search the second- and third-tier Rent-a-Wreck companies for lower age thresholds and be prepared to have someone sign with you. Although I have signed notes with interns, I prefer not to (ever since one fell into arrears on his apartment). Don't ask an editor. Have a relative co-sign.

We hired another intern who could not drive (his editor, the same one who had the other intern, has legitimate questions about my thoroughness), but he was so resourceful, we didn't find out for weeks. He got around—somehow—and came back with stories. We think he used buses and cabs and kept it to himself.

Phones, computers, and automobiles

You can shoot yourself in the foot with a gun, or you can do it with a computer.

Here's how: Use your office computer to play Solitaire, shop online or instant message all your friends: "Yo, CK—am on my summer gig. It's way easier than I thought, tho. Had orientation yest'day and this old dude spent 45 minutes telling me how to do e-mail. LMAO."

All newspapers provide staffers with tools to help them do their jobs. At minimum, there is a computer and a phone on the desk. There might also be pagers, phone cards, cell phones, camera equipment, the use of company cars, and reimbursement for expenses. Permanent hires might also get company credit cards.

Not all of us are wizards at keeping track of a lot of stuff. (Has anyone seen my car keys?) But if you're being trusted like a professional, even in small ways, you should act like a professional. Being sloppy with these tools might be interpreted as a sign that you're sloppy with your journalism, and that can be a career-killer.

Jayson Blair, who disgraced himself by inventing and stealing material for stories in the *New York Times,* showed similar behavior in the way he handled *Times* equipment and expenses. Careless disregard for the company car, telephone, or computer might be warning signs that the person has the same cavalier attitude about the rules of journalism.

You work hard to be respected for your honesty, accuracy, and integrity. Don't trash your reputation with a handful of parking tickets, carelessness or petty dishonesty.

Every newspaper has its own policies. Ask what they are and follow them to a T. If you break one, own up immediately and clear your record. Do not try to hide your mistakes. These are policies you might expect:

Computers: Newspapers have two primary concerns about their computers. One is that the things run smoothly, the other is that they are used just for business. To keep viruses out, the company may have rules against opening attachments or downloading programs that the newspaper has not approved of or purchased licenses for. Do not install anything on the newsroom computer without checking first. Do not even try to install instant messenger programs or log into personal e-mail accounts without asking. Technology editors have found that these can poke holes in the newsroom's firewall, making the system vulnerable. Imagine how naïve you're going to look if, while using your mad computer skills, you download the attachment that crashes the newsroom computer system on deadline. Keep a squeaky clean line between work and personal pursuits. Anyone walking by can see what is on your screen. If you shop online, people see it. If you play games, people see it. And let's not even talk about porn. Assume that everything you do on the office computer is being simulcast to the editors, backed up, archived, and will be permanently retrievable. Because it is. (OK, I made up that part about being simulcast. They probably won't use that feature.) Do you really want everyone to know that you spend two hours a day e-mailing friends? I once told an intern to kill a blog, written at work, that implicated that intern and others in activities that would have been embarrassing for all. If read by a strict publisher, it could have pulled the plug on the internship.

Laptops: Like photo equipment and cell phones, these things can sprout legs and run away. If laptops tend to do that more frequently while they are in your care, expect to go without them. You can also expect to get some evil looks from staff members who need to use equipment you have lost. Keep a hand—not just your eye—on expensive equipment, or keep it locked down. Photographers, the trunk of a car is not meant to be overnight storage for your gear.

A harried sports writer covering the Olympics set his laptop on top of his rental car, threw his notes and other junk into the rental and drove off. He soon realized he had forgotten to put the laptop inside. He pulled over and looked on top of the car. No laptop. He drove back to the stadium parking lot. No laptop in sight.

"Hey, officer, did anyone find a laptop computer out here?"

"Small package in a black case with a shoulder strap?"

"Yes!"

"Out here in the parking lot?"

"Yes, great!"

"Oh. It looked suspicious. The bomb squad blew it up."

How would you like to explain that one?

Desk phones: Obviously, using company phones for personal business is a no-no. Everyone understands the occasional call about personal business, but chit-chatting with friends around the country or arranging your next vacation is out. In addition to tying up what is meant to be your business line, this indicates you're not all that serious about your work. Chat on your own time, on your own phone. If you have to make extensive arrangements for something important and can do it only during your work hours, clear it ahead of time with your editor, do it on a break, and try to find a place that is more private than the middle of the newsroom

Pagers and cell phones: Obviously, every call made on or to a cell phone generates a record, and this record goes to the owner of the cell phone—the newspaper. Be ready to answer for every call on your cell phone. These are issued as much to help your editors do their jobs—by keeping up with you—as to help you do your job. If the company gives you a pager and you never respond to pages, they'll ask whether it is something with the pager—or with you. Keep these charged up or in batteries and keep them near you. It is unprofessional for journalists to be unavailable. Exception: For religious reasons, some people cannot

The Edge ———————————————————————————

Get to know your way around the newspaper's Intranet. It likely has a bulletin board for regular updates and it probably has a staff directory that will let you look up fellow staffers by name, home address, department, or by their picture. This can help you find out who lives near you or who that person was that you met yesterday. It might also include all the expense forms and policies that people forgot to tell you about.

use devices like these at certain times. Explain ahead of time. Most editors will get it.

Company cars: Some newspapers maintain a fleet of cars that staffers can use to go out on business. Business does not mean grocery shopping or having lunch with friends. Going out to lunch will not seem very businesslike if a reporter who needs a car to go out on a story is caught short. Using a company car means having a valid driver's license in your possession and it may mean having up-to-date auto insurance. These things are so basic—why am I even saying them? Guess.

Use good manners when you use a company car. The next person in it may be the person who sits next to you—or who signs your time sheet. Do not leave the gas tank empty or the backseat full of junk.

Parking tickets: You can win a Pulitzer Prize during your internship, but it is far more likely that the only citation you get will be for parking. Some newspapers will reimburse staff members for tickets acquired in the pursuit of journalism. If they do, and if that's how you won those citations, turn them in right away with a note of explanation. Sometimes, prompt payment of a parking ticket brings down the price. It will say on the ticket. If you sit on tickets, they get more expensive. If you get a ticket for being dumb—I got one for parking right outside the front door for "just a minute" and then forgetting to move my car—consider this a course in memory enhancement and pay for it yourself.

I was surprised—and not in a pleasant way—when our budget manager told me that an intern, then long gone, had amassed a mittful of parking tickets with company cars and had told no one at the paper. The paper was stuck with tickets and late fees. I had egg on my face and that intern cannot get a positive recommendation from me. It's not just that he left us holding these tickets. That's only money. The real problem is that he made me doubt that he is ethical, honest, and responsible.

Schedules

I can just imagine the wave of panic that flushed through one intern when the metro editor called him on a Sunday and asked whether he was coming to work.

"I didn't know I was supposed to work. I never had a Sunday before."

Check the schedule. Check the schedule. Check the schedule.

While you may start an internship with Monday-Friday shifts, the better you do and the longer you're there, the more likely it is you'll get thrown some nights and weekends.

Find out where the schedules are posted, how far in advance they go up and how susceptible they are to change. Most internships occur in the summer and can have funny schedules around holidays: Memorial Day, the Fourth of July, and, for later internships, Labor Day.

Days off

If you need to ask for certain days off, do it as far in advance as possible. If you are given the time before the internship begins, save the e-mail and remind someone when you show up. Expect that days off will be unpaid. Permanent staffers accrue vacation days and sick days. Interns do not. You might, however, ask if you can make up missed days so that you get the full experience and pay that the newspaper offered you.

Nights and weekends

Smart interns look for opportunities to work nights and weekends. These are times when staffing is short and when anyone who is available may have a crack at the big story. Sometimes, an intern winds up with a Page One story just for being the go-to person when news breaks.

An intern at the *Boston Globe* got the sweet assignments by going in early. He figured out that, although interns were not scheduled in until 10 a.m., some editors were in more than an hour before that and were ready to assign breaking stories. He went in early and got the choicest assignments. Some of the other interns got their ire up. They should have gotten themselves up.

Start time

Obviously, you don't want to be late for work. It's unprofessional. Yet so many of us schedule ourselves so tightly that we leave no room for the unexpected. What if you customarily planned to be at work thirty minutes early every day?

Overtime

Workdays generally have seven and a half to eight hours of work with a break for lunch. Weeks customarily have 37.5 to 40 hours. Ask about the newspaper's policy and how to submit for overtime. Overtime pay is typically time-and-a-half. For example, if you usually make $10 an hour and work an hour of overtime, you would be paid $15 before taxes for that hour. In a lot of newsrooms, the rule is that overtime is paid only if it is approved by an editor in advance. So, just ask, "This will take me past the end of my shift. Do you mean you want me to work this on overtime?"

In some shops, the editors may give you "comp time"—paid time off—in lieu of money.

You certainly should ask for overtime if you are called in on a day off. If you are, you might be entitled for a full day of overtime pay, even if they need you for just a few hours. The tricky part of overtime is knowing what to do on a daily basis.

For short, optional stays to "babysit" a story or artwork into the newspaper, people don't customarily put in for overtime, as it has not been pre-approved and is not really necessary. Fractions of an hour are not often submitted, either. A person who turns in for ten minutes of overtime on this day and five on that will get a reputation as a clock-watcher. So can a person who springs up at the quitting bell and dashes for the door. You want neither to work for free if you're in a paid position nor seem to be eager to get out the door. Take your time, make sure your work is done, check out with your editors.

Overtime should show up on your paycheck as a separate line or category. Save your pay stubs from week to week so you can note changes. Ask about any changes you don't understand.

Staying on track

First day

Yay! First day!

The Edge ———————————————————————

Some people are nice to the bosses and dismissive of the administrative staff. Big mistake. In most newsrooms, administrative people have the longest tenure and can be the most helpful. And smart bosses ask for their impressions of the interns.

So, what do you take, what will you do and what should you expect?

First days of internships can be awesome or awful. The experience is not entirely under your control, but here's what you can do to nudge things toward awesome.

Read the newspaper thoroughly before you go the office that first day and carry it in with you. You're likely to meet people who helped create it, and someone might ask you what you thought of it. Be ready with some specifics.

Get there early—a good half hour early—and know whom to ask for, but plan to wait in the lobby until starting time. After all, you may be arriving before your editor does. Smart people make a dry run a day in advance to see where the building and parking are without asking their new bosses a lot of questions that may make them seem needy.

What to wear

Dress professionally. You can't go too far wrong if you are a little overdressed on your first day. People will understand. Plus, you can sometimes take a little starch out of a starched collar. Lose the tie or jacket if you need to come down a notch. If you go in under-dressed, you will not be able to catch up. If your work will take you to formal places like courtrooms or corporate boardrooms, dress up. How sad it would be if you lost out on a good story because you were not dressed and ready to go.

On that first day, pay attention to what people in your department wear so you'll have a better idea of the clothing culture. People who are inclined to treat interns like kids can be influenced by the way you

JobsPage in My Pocket

Essentials for first day of work
• Social Security card
• passport, other proof of citizenship or work permit, just in case
• driver's license
• proof of auto insurance
• quarters, in case you have to use a metered parking spot
• notebook

dress and carry yourself. Dress more like the editors rather than the kookiest person you see and you'll command more respect. (Kooky dressers, I mean no disrespect. I like people who liven up the newsroom by showing a little personality. But know that not all newsrooms and not all editors appreciate that.)

Thoughtful editors will have made a plan for someone to take you to the cafeteria or out for lunch that first day. Even nice editors get waylaid when news strikes. So pack something in your bag or purse that you can grab if news events or inattention mean there is no lunch break. You'll feel silly if you walk in with a brownbag lunch and they say, "Hey, c'mon, we're not going to let you eat a sack lunch on your first day." So, be prepared, but don't be obvious about it.

Take notes. You're going to meet a lot of people and you're going to get a lot of instructions. There probably will be forms to fill out, an I.D. to pose for, a news meeting to attend, computer training, and a tour of the newsroom. You can pretend you're memorizing all this, but they'll know you didn't when you come back the second day. It is natural for journalists to take notes.

Find out where they post the schedule in your department. Check it at least once a week throughout your internship.

First week

Before you get through the orientation, you're likely to want to do some actual work. Internships are brief and we want to make the most of them. Here's how to hit the ground running.

Arrive at the paper with some ideas for stories or photos and about different experiences you'd like to have. Don't pitch them on your first day. Hold onto them until the editors are receptive. They likely have some initial plans for you. Good journalists, though, have a store of ideas they can pitch when the assignments run out or toward the mundane. Assigning editors appreciate people who offer story ideas. People who want to make successful story pitches read the newspaper closely to see what's running, what editors are looking for, and when stories trigger ideas for other stories.

Take the initiative. There are a lot of people at the newspaper who can help you, but they have jobs to do, too. Don't interpret lack of attention as lack of interest. They're just busy. But they'll make time for you.

If you don't understand something, ask about it. If you want to know how you're doing, ask. If you want to try something new . . . you get the idea. If you've never spent a day with a newspaper photographer, worked on a copy desk or seen the presses roll, this is your chance. So, speak up. Remember: Most people are flattered to have someone ask for their opinion or help.

Mid-internship

Don't be surprised if you hit a lull or a slump after a few weeks. Maybe it's biorhythms. Maybe it's the alignment of the stars. Don't worry if it happens to you. It probably just means that some of the jitters have worn off, or you've worked through the initial assignments that were waiting for you. Continued hard work will get you through. Veterans have slumps, too.

Ask your editor for a midpoint assessment. Set an appointment a few days in advance so the editor knows that this is important. Save your editor some searching and hand over a collection of the work you'd like to talk about. Ask about strengths as well as weaknesses and do not interrupt criticism to defend yourself. You can't learn while you're talking.

Begin to think about your next internship or job. Which clips will you use, based on your talk with an editor or mentor? What sort of work do you still need to do to make this a well-rounded internship?

Start cultivating a reference. You should be able to list a good reference from every job you do. Who will it be here? A good reference is someone who hires and evaluates employees, who has first-hand knowledge of your work, who is articulate and, of course, enthusiastic about you. Once you have identified some people—let's hope one is your editor—let them in on your decision-making and the stories behind the stories. The better they know you, the stronger the reference.

Be sure you're getting out of the newsroom. Yes, it is fun to hang around the newsroom with other journalists, but geez, get a life and get out into the world. Good journalists never stop learning about their readers and communities. So, if you're going to serve your readers well, especially if you're new to town, meet as many of them as you can.

Have fun. Yeah, that's right. Have fun on your internship. Fun is important. After all, why do you think we got into newspapering?

Final weeks

You'll be in your final weeks before you know it. Ten months to get an internship, ten weeks to work it. Here's how to polish off your internship.

As one new hire told me, "It's all about the clip." So, get yours. On your own or with the help of the library staff, get a paper copy and a digital copy of what you want to take with you. You don't need to get a copy of everything—just the good stuff—and you need only one actual clipping of your best work. While you're doing this, see if you can come up with any good statistics that might boost your résumé: "I wrote seventeen front-page headlines." "One day, I had the lead photo on the front page, the local section, and one on the front of sports." "I wrote fifty stories and had no corrections."

It will be much easier to score your clips while you're at the paper with free access to the computer archives and back copies.

You've worked hard to make the right impression; now it's time to find out what impression you've made. We just talked about the qualities of a good reference. To seal it up ask, "If someone were to ask you for a reference on me, what would you say?" Besides nailing down your reference, you might ask for a letter of recommendations that includes information specific to you for a generic employer.

Final evaluation: Ask if one is coming. If not, ask for one. In many cases, editors do exit interviews with departing employees to see what they can learn. You should use that opportunity the same way.

Get the names and contact information you'll need. Take a copy of the office directory. That is proprietary (inside) information, but it

---

JobsPage in My Pocket

Questions for your final appraisal:

How did I do, generally?
How was my productivity?
How was my work? Where should I improve?
Did I show enough initiative and hustle?
Do I respond well to editing and suggestions?
What kind of work experience should I have next?
Which jobs do you think will lead to my greatest success?

is OK for employees to have, provided they don't share it with anyone else—certainly not a competing newsroom.

Any unexplored parts of the paper?

Last check: Make sure your immediate supervisor, the department or newsroom manager, and the person who handled payroll checks all have the address you'll be using after your internship.

Return equipment such as cell phones or pagers and your company I.D. Don't let an equipment malfunction stand in the way of a positive reference.

Guest: Intern confidential: How to really make the most of your internship

By THEOLA S. LABBÉ
Reporter
The Washington Post

Dear Interns:

It's early spring and you get the call. "Hi, I'm So-and-So from the So-and-So publication and we'd like to offer you a summer internship."

You almost can't believe it. Months of sending out résumés, cover letters, and clips, networking with recruiters at job fairs, and working hard in your journalism classes has finally paid off.

So, with a hearty yes, you accept the internship, and excitedly count the days until you can walk into your new employer and "Be aggressive!" You plan to: thoroughly research your new town so you can come armed with story ideas, badger your editor for work once you get there, and help out on other stories in any and every way possible. A ready-made formula for success, right?

Well, not quite. What journalism teachers, and even recruiters don't tell you is that the minute you arrive, you first have to understand how the place works—the big picture—before you can be the star intern. Who is the well-dressed man who walks across the newsroom with an air of confidence? When do the editors get together and decide the front page? And from where is everyone getting those fresh slices of pizza and free soda?

Once you know how the big picture works in your newsroom, you're well on your way to fitting yourself into the frame. This doesn't mean changing your personality in order to fit in. Instead, with your insight into the way things work, and of course, your talent (why else would you be there?) you'll stand out as the smart intern with realistic expectations.

It's more than just being aggressive. From my own internship experience, I've come up with five suggestions that can help you make the most of your internship.

Know your editors' schedule and responsibilities

I like to call this one "Stalking your editor." Do you know what time your editor arrives at and leaves work? How many other employees does your editor supervise? When is your editor in a meeting? Common sense should tell you not to approach your editor at 2:20 p.m. when there is a 2:30 news meeting, or to pitch your feature story idea about stray rabbits the day of a plane crash. They don't have time to listen. Recognize when your editor has time to talk and adjust your plans accordingly. If that means coming in at 8:30 a.m. or staying way after your deadline has passed to catch their ear, so be it. Otherwise, you'll get less attention and probably less out of the internship.

Get to know your boss' boss

Your editor is under pressure to meet certain expectations from his/her boss, and these expectations will undoubtedly affect the kind of assignments that you do. If other editors want more stories from the suburbs, your editor will tell you to start combing the towns. You can make things easier for both of you by jotting down the concerns voiced by executive and managing editors in meetings. Then try to come up with ways to address those concerns during your internship. You'll be a valuable asset if you're aware of the larger issues that plague the publication as a whole, not just your department or beat.

Theola S. Labbé is a reporter at The Washington Post and won the National Association of Black Journalists' 2004 Young Journalist Award for her reporting in Iraq. She was a Detroit Free Press intern in 1998.

Talk to your co-workers

I sat next to a Pulitzer Prize winning journalist for six weeks and didn't even know it. Many of the people around you are seasoned, award-winning pros who can give you story ideas, advice on how to improve your work, or entertain you with their hard-knock stories. Make sure to talk to other departments, too. Reporters should know copy editors, photographers should know production staff, etc. All of your co-workers have something to teach you simply because they've been working there longer than you have. Don't feel bad about being a novice; your gift to them is that you bring a new way of looking at issues that your co-workers have long since grown tired of. So be sure to share your ideas with other people, and let them enlighten you.

Find out who takes care of the paperwork, and make friends fast

Say you worked a couple of hours of overtime, but have no idea where to get the OT form. Whoever takes care of administrative tasks can probably tell you where to get the form and how to fill it out, along with where you can go to cash your check, file for story expenses, or get a replacement ID badge. It doesn't quite have anything to do with your reporting skills, but the less time you spend fretting about your lost ID, the more time you have to work on getting an A1 story.

The miscellaneous, but still important stuff

Listen to a news radio station before you come to work—you'll be up to speed and ready to pounce on any breaking news story the minute you arrive in the newsroom . . . If you still can't get time with your editor, or things aren't going as well as you would like, ask them to lunch . . . Write a memo to your editor midway through your internship outlining what you've done so far and what you would like to do . . . Be sure to chat with the recruiter (or the person who hired you) during the summer to honestly let them know how things are going. . . Try to get a written evaluation midway through, and at the end of your internship . . . Work hard and ask questions . . . Oh, and lastly, be sure to send thank-you cards to everyone who lent you a hand.

That's it! Hey, don't sweat it. You'll be great.

Sincerely,

Theola S. Labbé ✳

7

From Internship to Job

Internships are over in the wink of an eye. Almost as soon as you get there, you're gone. At some newspapers, internships have been cut from twelve weeks to ten as editors have tried to deal with budget cuts without losing positions.

Even before students start their internships they ask, "How soon should I start the search for a job?"

That depends. People who will return from their internships to college should not do any heavy job searching during their internships. It is too early and could get in the way of doing their best.

People in their last internships should not start looking for the next step for a while. It takes time to learn the paper, its opportunities, and what it can teach. Someone who starts looking as soon as they land will be missing out.

The only people who truly need to start looking during the first few months of taking internships are graduates. They should start looking seriously about halfway through the internship. The search should be managed so it does not get in the way of doing a good job and it can become more intense as the internship winds down.

The first half of the internship should be dedicated to doing quality work. That work could open a door leading from the internship right into a job, or it could be the thing that persuades editors to use their influence to help you land a post-internship job.

The first step for people in the job search is to have a frank talk with the editors.

- If something were to open here, would I be a competitive candidate for it?
- Do you have or expect any openings?

146

- If I would not be a credible candidate here at this time, can you tell what I still need to learn or do to get there?
- Can you suggest some good places for me to go to next?
- Do you have any contacts there?

Do not base your success as an intern on whether you land a job. Internships are steppingstones. While newspapers do use them as try-outs, they are using them as auditions for eventual jobs—not immediate ones. And it just makes sense that a sharp, well-prepared newspaper that recruits will have candidates who are more experienced and qualified than interns who have just started working there in the past few months.

When you move from an internship to a job, you are going through a big transition, and it can be frustrating—even for the best. Imagine that you are one of the best:

You've worked hard, held a series of internships with successively larger newspapers, are on a first-name basis with some of the best recruiters in the nation and, now that you're finally ready to graduate into a job . . . nada.

Recruiters who seemed happy to take your call and big newspapers that fought with each other to get you to intern there are now drying up. "Good luck," we say. "Call us in a few years." "Keep in touch."

What gives? How did you go from red-hot to ice-cold?

It's simple.

Think of yourself as a playing card (an ace, not a joker). When you graduate from college, you move from the top half of the internship deck to the bottom half of the job deck. While you used to be one of the most accomplished people in college, you now become one of the least experienced people out of college.

Nothing changed about you. You graduated into a higher stratum. You had worked to be at the top of the collegiate pool. Now, you've got to start over. While college students with four years of internship experience are impressive, candidates with years of permanent experience might logically be better candidates for jobs.

Reference grooming

Much of the work you do to get an internship will be like the work you do to get a job. The résumé, the cover letter, clips, and perhaps an autobiographical essay—these will all be expected when you apply for a job. The key difference between internship applications and job applications is that interviews, references, and testing become more important. Your past performance will become more important than impressions of your future potential.

Guest: Get your net working

By DON HUDSON
Managing Editor
The Clarion-Ledger

Approach your job search as you'd approach the job, considering these basic elements of journalism:

Source development. Make this priority No. 1. Build that source base from coast to coast, from region to region. Why? You need to know about the culture of every major media organization.

How do you get started? Well, you can build industry sources through attending job fairs and external training (API, Maynard, Poynter, IRE, etc.). But don't wait for your supervisor to nominate you for a training session or job fair; search Web sites and figure out how to do things on the cheap. Or, figure out how to get into these sessions free.

Once accepted, go in with a good idea of what you hope to accomplish. Soak up the expertise of everyone and everything in the room. Pass out those business cards. Take advantage of every social gathering.

At job fairs, work the room. It doesn't matter what type of job fair it is—it could be for business reporters, for editors or for minority journalists. Just show up, meet and greet folks.

The Edge ──────────────────────────────────
Before you use someone as a reference, ask them, "If I were to use you as a reference, what would you say about me?" If their answer is positive, specific, and articulate, then ask if you may use them. Otherwise, don't The danger in simply asking, "May I use you as a reference?" is that many people will simply consent, even if they have nothing good to say about you.

If your employer doesn't give you time off for a fair, take time off and go on your own. Drop your card and work samples off at every booth. Make sure you get quality face time with each recruiter. Make sure that recruiter remembers you—for all the right reasons. Make sure you're firm, decisive, energetic, knowledgeable about the industry, and bring expertise to the table regarding your specialty. Tell folks you'd like to follow up in a couple of weeks.

Knowledge of the subject. If you're headed to Poynter, know the background of all the presenters. This helps during social gatherings. Be knowledgeable about the lead subject and at least literate on all other topics. Bottom line: Go in prepared and be ready to impress.

If you're applying for a job, drop the "To Whom" . . . gibberish from your cover letter. Know to whom you're supposed to apply, whether a recruiter, the managing editor, an assistant ME or the editor. Never send your packet to human resources unless instructed. Know that paper's background, its circulation, its claim to excellence, and perhaps even goals set for that year by top editors. Be prepared to tell editors why you're right for this position; offer at least three reasons why they should hire you. One reason should be teamwork; you have to be a team player to survive the politics of any newsroom.

Follow up/cold contacts. Never lose contact. As soon as you return from your trip, drop an e-mail and say thanks. Point out the good things you gained from the trip. Point out areas where you need to improve. Say you'd like to stay in touch and send work samples every three months or so.

Another possibility: Consider cold-calling or cold-e-mailing one of your favorites. If you have a favorite designer, writer, or editor out there, reach out. Send a note or packet and ask that person to critique

Don Hudson, managing editor of The Clarion-Ledger in Jackson, Mississippi, helps recruit for Gannett Co., which is based in McLean, Virginia.

your work. If your long-term goal is to become a publisher, find one you admire and ask that person to help plot your future. ✳

Schmooze-free networking

Many people say that networking makes them feel a little sleazy.

They feel that schmoozing is selfish and that people who do it are just using others.

That is not networking.

Networking, done right, is not about getting what you can out of other people. The best networkers do not do it for themselves. They network because they genuinely like to help people.

That's right, proper networking is for others, not for yourself.

Each of us has a network. It includes relatives, friends, people who live near us, and people we work with. But not everyone is seen as a networker. The people who have that reputation tend to be the people who have connections to an extensive number and range of people. A quilter can know a large number of other people who also quilt. Quilting circles, shows, and Web sites can connect them. A person who plays recreational volleyball in a couple of leagues can know a lot of people from many different backgrounds. They can use those networks to help each other find information, techniques, goods and services, and to welcome new people into the network. Sometimes, some of this goodwill comes back to them, of course, but they tend not to form these relationships just to become better quilters or volleyball players. There is nothing sleazy about what they're doing.

One more thing about people whose networks help them find jobs: News about opportunities tends to come from people they know—but not all that well. Your closest friends tend to know what you also know. Fresh news comes from people with whom you have weaker attachments and who operate in circles outside of your own. Some of the key research in this area comes from sociologist Mark Granovetter, who found that more successful job leads come from our looser attachments, rather than the tighter ones. It's all in his 1974 study, "Getting a Job."

Journalists, quite naturally have networks, too. As people move from place to place and as they meet each other at conferences or in online discussions, these networks can easily span the country or the globe.

And healthy networking leads people to help each other with an introduction, the word on something interesting they've read or heard that might help someone else succeed. The good networker works for the good of the others.

No two people have the same network. The people in your network do not all know each other. One of the most helpful things you can do is to introduce one person in your network to someone else, making connections that will help them. This is networking. It helps out the people you're connected to and makes your network stronger by connecting more and more people—with their accompanying networks—to each other.

Every time you add someone to your network, you bring in someone—and all their connections—who could help the people you're already connected to.

In addition to dropping the selfish, me-first approach to networking, these are a few strategies you can use to network and still hold your head up:

- Be yourself. People spot phonies a mile away. Don't suck up.
- Be sincere about what you are doing. If you need help, ask for it.
- Let the other person be who he or she really is, too.
- Go for sustained contacts with key people, not just a lot of one-time contacts with a big number of people. Don't try to make it grow too fast, and look for long-lasting connections.

Link to build relationships. A network can grow like a field of weeds—which is not all bad—or like a garden that you prune, water and nurture. (Be careful how you spread that fertilizer.) Be systematic about maintaining your network, and it will be a fuller, healthier garden.

Some people to cultivate for your garden:

- Someone for skills
- Someone for managing office politics
- Someone for advice on your career
- Someone for personal and family advice
- A friend to whom you can safely vent, but who will push you toward finding solutions, too.

People I will add to my network	What they bring
_____	_____
_____	_____
_____	_____
_____	_____

Guest: **Have sound roots and reach for the stars**

By CEDRIC BRYANT
Manager/College and Professional Recruiting
Gannett

Journalist: a person who keeps a journal, diary, or other record of daily events.

The mere definition says it all. But as our world evolves, the methods, technology, and approach to keeping a record of daily events must change also.

Young journalists must think in the broadest possible ways about how to present information. These thoughts must include multiple platforms of delivery while preserving the core fundamentals of journalism.

The Edge ————————————————————————————
If you build this way to strengthen your network and the people in it, rather than just to help yourself, a strange thing will happen. Your good work will come back to help you in unexpected ways. University of Michigan Business School Prof. Wayne Baker explains it in a book titled *Achieving Success Through Social Capital: Tapping Hidden Resources in Your Personal and Business Networks.* He calls the helpful nature of networks unselfishly built the law of reciprocity. The book explains it in greater depth, of course.

Here are three pieces of advice to help young journalists prepare for their careers.

Master the basics. You should be inquisitive, proficient with Associated Press style, familiar with current events, and have a strong grasp of grammar. These items are the foundation for all aspiring journalists. These are also things that you can control by the amount of dedication and focus you put into mastering them. This also applies to communication skills, portfolio presentations, and job interviewing.

A good communicator possesses outstanding written and oral skills and knows how to use them effectively.

Even though your résumé took you hours to write, hiring managers will typically spend less than one minute reviewing it. If your résumé has any glaring errors, employers will waste no time in deleting it. To ensure your résumé gets proper attention, avoid any potential mistakes. Ask at least five people to proof it for you.

According to a CareerBuilder survey, the No. 1 mistake interviewees make relates to how they communicate. The second most common way candidates flub their interviews is with what they do.

Many of these mistakes are the result of being unprepared and knowing nothing about the job or company. Others are because candidates don't listen to the questions being asked or try to bluff their way through technical questions. Some stem from a lack of common sense or courtesy.

Develop a working knowledge of technology and how it can be used in the news delivery process.

Cedric Bryant joined Gannett in 1993 at The Times in Shreveport, Louisiana, where he worked as the education and human relations editor and later as the sports editor. He joined Gannett's corporate recruiting team in 1995. He currently works as the manager/college and professional recruiting. He oversees the college, entry-level and professional recruiting across all disciplines. Prior to joining Gannett, Cedric worked at the Greensboro (North Carolina) News & Record. Bryant is a 1990 graduate of North Carolina Agricultural and Technical State University. He is a member of the National Association of Minority Media Executives, National Association of Black Journalists and National Association of Hispanic Journalists.

"It would appear that we have reached the limits of what is possible to achieve with computer technology, although one should be careful with such statements, as they tend to sound pretty silly in five years."

—John Von Neumann, 1949

Von Neumann, a noted mathematician and physicist, appears to have had an inkling of what you know well. Computer technology is constantly evolving.

You should strive to have at least a working familiarity with as many of the software programs used in newsrooms as possible. There is often a commonality among many programs, so a working knowledge is extremely helpful.

Computer literacy is a must for any aspiring journalist. Working at your campus newspaper or doing summer internships can present opportunities to gain these skills.

Keep an open mind and be receptive to change. Change is in the air and news organizations are trying many new, exciting approaches to the traditional business model.

You should embrace this and bring the same approach to your own work. A positive attitude will take you a long way in life. Approach work with a high energy level, tons of enthusiasm, a zest for living, and the determination to be the very best at whatever you do.

Enthusiasm is infectious. It is motivating and drives others to higher levels of productivity and success. Show your enthusiasm every chance you get and you dramatically increase your chances of being noticed.

This is a great time to be entering the journalism profession and exciting for our industry. ✻

Is it whom you know or what you know?

Job-seekers in every field have spent a lot of time wondering, debating, and worrying about that question. Here's the answer:

It is neither whom you know nor what you know. It is both.

If you do not know and cannot learn how to do the job, you will fail. If you do not know anyone who can help you get the job, or do not ask the ones you do know, you may not get to use your skills.

You need both.

Ask the same question about reporting. Do good reporters succeed because of what they know or whom they know? They have to have both. A reporter without sources is as weak as a reporter without skills. Good reporters use every lead they have to get a story. So do successful job-seekers.

So why are we hung up on that question?

We get stuck there because the question makes a false distinction between honorable, honest job-hunting and something sleazier. In that cardboard cutout world, respectable hiring is solely about competence. Underhanded deal-making is all about the connections. When we fail to get ahead, we blame it on our lack of contacts. When others pass us by, we credit their connections to protect our pride. It's how we comfort ourselves when someone else gets something that we feel we deserve more.

Get over all that.

Getting hired is about competence and connections. Both. Know your stuff and have a good network. Don't be hard on other people for using their connections, and don't be reluctant to use your own.

Relationship building

This is just an observation, but I think it is instructive.

One fall, I received twenty-one internship applications from students in Columbia University's graduate school of journalism. In January, I went to New York City, where Columbia is located, for *Newsday*'s excellent job fair. The book of registered job-seekers contained résumés of eighteen Columbia grad students. Four were from people whose applications I had recently read. Here was an opportunity for them to build on their initital contacts.

Over two days, I interviewed thirty-six candidates. But of the four who had applied to us and registered for this job fair, only one came around to interview. I did, however, meet three new Columbia students.

So, I return to New York in April, for a job fair organized by Columbia itself, right inside the journalism building. By now, I had received applications from or interviewed twenty-five of the people who would likely be at this job fair. By coincidence, I interviewed twenty-five on that day in April. How many of the original twenty-five were in this group of twenty-five? Just one—the same guy who had interviewed in January. There was almost no follow-through. One student alone demonstrated the value of persistence. Although I recognized some of the students I had seen in January, they did not seem to recognize me when I said hello.

I was seeing where the shotgun approach to job-hunting misses. By applying everywhere and concentrating nowhere, these students, some of the best in the country, were missing an opportunity to get beyond a superficial job search.

Most job-seekers know not to burn bridges, but they might know how to build them. Bridges are not built from the middle and generally not all from one end, but from both ends until they meet in the middle. When a job candidate sends out a letter or a recruiter makes a campus visit, that is a start, from one side or the other. The two sides will not connect unless both sides take several steps toward the conclusion of the project.

Let's go back to that *Newsday* job fair and meet a bridge-builder. She had graduated from a program that does not have a big name and, as no one had been schooling her and pushing her, she had not had an internship. On her own, she had learned that getting one would help her get started.

She had some clips from school and some community papers, but she had been working outside of journalism in the eight months since graduation. She kept knocking on our door. She traveled from Detroit to Washington, D.C., to a job fair in August and interviewed with dozens of newspapers there—including ours. In November, still trying to get in, she came to our job fair in Detroit and talked to us. In January, she traveled to New York for the *Newsday* job fair. At every stop, she waited in line to interview with the *Free Press*. When she showed up in New York, I had just learned that we would hire some winter some interns immediately. It was a fluke. I told her to go out into the job fair, see what she could get, and to come back at the end of it.

She followed directions and came back with the usual story—lots of encouragement, but no one thought she had enough experience. So, I offered her an internship on the spot. I almost never do that, but by now, I knew a lot about her and knew that she was serious about working for us.

Now, was this a case of being in the right place at the right time? Or knowing the right people? Or persistence? Or being ready when opportunity presented itself? It was a case of a hard-working person using all those variables.

The transition to permanent hire

Each year, a few lucky people get turned from interns into permanent employees. Some candidates seek out internships where this can happen, passing up larger newspapers where it probably won't. And it's no wonder that a few get offers, as most newspapers use internships as dress rehearsals.

If the paper where you are interning offers you a permanent job, recognize that you are once again in a decision window and negotiate the details as you would for any full-time offer. Take the transition casually and you may regret it later.

First, ask about the pay. You should get paid more as a permanent hire than you were getting paid as an intern. "How much?" the editors may ask. Answer the question with a question, "Well, how much do you pay permanent staffers?" Expect them to give you a range or a starting salary, but do not let them leave you in the awkward position of naming your price. Chances are, they have something in mind and you neither want to lowball yourself nor price yourself out of the job.

Your best negotiating tools at this point are the good work you have done—that's what got you the offer—and the amount of time you have already spent as a full-time journalist. Start with your three months working for them. Add the time from prior internships. Do not count time you spent working for the college paper. If you can scrape together six months or more in professional newsrooms, ask whether that experience can lift you into a higher bracket.

If accepting a job means sending for the stuff you didn't move because you had not planned to stay there, or if you will now need to buy a car, say so. Do not bring in your student loans or credit card debt. Those kinds of needs do not typically lead to higher salaries. I suppose that the college education helps make a person a suitable candidate for the paper and so the paper should help pay for that—but I have never seen that argument made and advise against it.

Try to get the money into your base pay, not in the form of bonuses. Your base pay builds, bonuses go away.

This shows how much better it is to get a $28,000 starting salary than a $25,000 starting salary with a $5,000 bonus. We'll figure a three percent raise each year for five years.

	Annual pay $25,000 base and $5,000 bonus	Annual pay $28,000 base No bonus
Year 1	$30,000	$28,000
Year 2	$25,750	$28,840
Year 3	$26,523	$29,705
Year 4	$27,318	$30,596
Year 5	$28,138	$31,514

The person who started with the nice bonus will make less than the other person from the second year on and after five years, the person without the bonus but with the higher base has out-earned the bonus-winner by almost $11,000. As long as they get raises of the same percentage, the gap between their salaries will continue to grow. Given a choice between a one-time bonus and a larger base, the larger base is almost always better.

In future negotiations with other employers, they will ask what you are getting paid, so you want to build the base, because this is what future raises are built on. A years-ago bonus will not be a factor in the negotiation.

When I explained this logic to another editor, he said, "You should get it in your base *and* get a bonus." More power to you!

Ask about moving expenses. You likely did not bring everything you own for your internship, but now you'll want it. Who is going to pay to move it? Keep your moving costs low—the newspaper won't expect to pay a fortune to move an intern's belongings—but ask for help. Remember that some moving expenses will be treated as income on your federal income taxes and you will have to pay taxes on some of the reimbursement. You may want to ask the company to increase the allowance to cover the taxes you'll owe. Some call this "grossing up" the moving expenses.

This next point is a little abstract, but it is worth asking about. Ask the editor what will be used as your official start date. You want your anniversary date to be as early as possible. Ask it to be when you began working at the newspaper—the first day of your internship—not the day the editors converted you to permanent status. Anniversary dates may be used to determine seniority, when you become eligible for an annual raise, when you get your evaluation or vacation. Hire dates can affect how soon you become eligible for health insurance. At the outset, this may be the most important reason for you to ask for the earliest possible start date.

If the end of your first day is going to bring a $2,000 raise, getting it three months earlier—on the anniversary of your internship start day rather than when you became a permanent hire—is, in effect, a onetime $500 advantage to you.

Next item to negotiate: paid vacations and holidays. The holidays should be standard across the staff, but you should know what they are. The pecking order for asking for vacation days or holidays off will favor the experienced, but ask what the rules are.

On vacation pay, ask how it is determined. It is usually a combination of seniority and the number of days worked. For example, a ten-year employee may get a paid vacation day for every fifteen days worked, while a new employee may get a day for every eighteen.

The formula can be confusing. So, ask for specifics. "If I am hired now, how many vacation days would I get this year, and how many would I get next year?" Beware of formulas that don't let you take any vacation time until the year after it is earned. That could mean you get no vacation days this year. If they matter to you, ask for some—or ask for some days between the end of your internship period and when you start work.

If you find you are not getting anywhere with wage negotiations or the start date, you might want to ask them to review your pay in six months, rather than a full twelve, promising to impress them so much they'll want to give you a raise.

Consider whether you want to negotiate for some training during your first year. Being so new, you likely would benefit from some training. Asking for it tells the editors that you are dedicated to improving your craft.

Incidentally, don't rely on your editors to be the sole investors in your training. This should be a large and permanent part of your career strategy and you should budget your own money for career development.

Guest: **Is this job right for you?**

By MELISSA JORDAN
Senior Editor for Recruiting and Training
San Jose Mercury News

So you have a job offer, or at least an interview.

How can you find out if it's the right job for you? Arm yourself with questions that can help you decide if the job, the newspaper, and the company are a good fit and a place where you can grow.

Whether it's an internship, a first job or a move anywhere along your career path, you should use your journalist's skills to learn as much as you can about the opportunity.

Here are some areas to explore with the hiring manager:

1. Feedback.

It seems like every newspaper these days aspires to have a "coaching culture." Delve into specifics to find out what that means. For example, ask: "How do you make sure employees get regular feedback?" An annual performance evaluation is one thing, but an ongoing emphasis on development is much more. Do supervisors receive training on how to coach? Are supervisors evaluated on the quality of their feedback?

2. Opportunities for growth.

Yes, you're talking about a specific job right now. But think about how it could help you reach your long-term goals. "What have been some typical next steps for people who were successful in this job?" "How does your newsroom identify and groom its best and brightest?" "Are there clear paths for moving up in the organization?"

Melissa Jordan *is senior editor for recruiting and training at the San Jose Mercury News.*

3. Training.

To reach your career goals, you need to constantly improve your skills. Part of that happens naturally on the job, and part requires training. "What kind of commitment does this newsroom have to professional development?" Get specific. "Can I see this year's in-house training schedule? Is there a tuition reimbursement program? Does the paper send people to seminars at places such as Poynter and API, and if so what is the selection process?"

4. Mission.

The newspaper probably has a mission statement, and it probably is heavy on generalities. Dig deeper into what it means. Talking about the newspaper's mission can help you decide if its priorities are a good match for your skills, interests, and passions. Is its focus largely local? Does the area have a defining attribute that drives coverage? What is its role in the community? Try an open-ended approach: "Can you talk about how the newspaper's mission affects some specific coverage decisions?"

5. Diversity.

If you value diversity as a core principle of journalism, make sure that any newspaper you go to does, too. Ask what priority the newspaper places on diversity—in coverage as well as in hiring. "What percentage of newsroom staff are women and people of color? What percentage of managers?" Other aspects of diversity are not as easily measured, but ask how the newspaper defines and embraces the concept. (Does it reflect people of all ages? Socioeconomic groups? Religious or political beliefs?) "Does the paper provide paid time off or pay registration and travel expenses for attending conventions such as the Asian American Journalists Association, the National Association of Black Journalists, the National Association of Hispanic Journalists, the Native American Journalists Association, the National Lesbian and Gay Journalists Association?

6. Culture.

Every newsroom has a culture; it's the personality of the place. Ask a few people to tell you about the culture, and see if you hear similar themes. Is it hard-charging? Laid-back? Competitive? Collaborative? Ask about specifics and examples for any adjective that's thrown out. What behaviors or actions are rewarded? Is there a culture committee or culture goals? A "writer's" paper? A "top-down" paper? Ask: "What does that mean? Give me some examples."

7. The job.
Find out as much as you can about the job you are seeking. Is there a written job description? Are there clear expectations? Is it a new position? If not, could you speak with the person who held the job? Is there an organizational chart for the department, so that you can see where this position fits into the big picture? Is there a specific yardstick that will let you know if you are achieving the goals of the job? (X number of stories on Page 1A in your first year? Work that wins prizes? Praise from readers? Impact in the community?)

8. The team.
Always ask if you can talk with people who would be your peers. They'll give you an in-the-trenches view that may be different from what the hiring manager tells you. Ask what it's like to do their job. What's the best thing about the paper? The worst thing? Whatever the most important issue is for you, ask them about it. ("Do you get to choose many of your own story ideas, or do you get more assignments from editors?" "Do copy editors have to call a reporter at home before changing anything in a story?" "Do photographers generate their own photo stories?" "Do you feel respected and valued at this paper?") It would be a red flag if your new editors were close to making you a job offer but would not connect you with future peers to interview.

9. The boss.
Of course you want to know about your immediate supervisor. But a word of caution: Don't fixate on finding the perfect supervisor, because *they change.* Frequently and without warning. Focus more on knowing the overall newsroom, the management philosophy, the nature of the work you'll be doing. You can find lots of advice once you're hired on the art of "managing up," to help you have the best possible relationship with any supervisor. (A good start: If it's not the immediate supervisor doing the hiring interview, ask if you could talk with him or her to find out more about the job. It'll show you are interested and give you a chance to sell yourself.)

10. The company.
Who owns the newspaper? Is it privately held? Publicly traded? Controlled by one family? What is its reputation in the industry? This is

another entire research project for you, but one that may be important in finding the right fit. Do your homework on the values and the quality of the parent company as well as of the newspaper itself. ✻

Guest: Good starts at small papers

By TED DANIELS
Editor and General Manager
Ashland Times-Gazette

My move from the comfort of a senior editor's position at a big-city metro to the editor's chair of my 12,500-circulation hometown daily elicited among my colleagues a range of reactions from bewilderment to envy.

But after nearly twenty-three years at *The Indianapolis Star,* during which time I filled a multitude of positions from copy editor to managing editor, I returned home to my small-town roots as editor of the *Ashland Times-Gazette* in North Central Ohio.

I moved from a newsroom of two-hundred seventy primarily mid-career journalists to a newsroom of fifteen mostly young, beginning journalists. The newsroom budget I managed in Indianapolis was more than four times the total revenues of my new newspaper. It's been a culture shock, but mostly good culture shock.

Readers, even complete strangers, aren't afraid to stop you in the grocery store or after church to tell you what they think about a particular story, editorial, or picture. While I was visiting my mother in the hospital late one evening, a nurse asked me, "Are you the Daniels

Ted Daniels, who has been the editor and general manager at the Ashland Times-Gazette in Ohio for five years, says that of his many varied duties and responsibilities during nearly twenty-three years at The Indianapolis Star (1978-2001), several stints of staff recruiting were among his favorites.

who is the editor of the paper?" When I said yes, bracing for the worst, she simply said, "Keep up the good work."

You see first-hand daily how your newspaper makes a real difference (most of the time good, sometimes bad) in your readers' lives.

This more intimate connection with readers is probably one of the reasons small newspapers make such great places to start journalism careers.

Far too many young journalists want to forego "paying their dues" working for little money at small newspapers and immediately jump to the glory, glamour, and big bucks of a big city metro. But ask any journalist who started at a small paper, and virtually all will tell you that they wouldn't trade that small newspaper experience for anything.

You get a range of experiences in a short period of time that can't be duplicated at bigger newspapers. While our reporters have beats, no one on our small staff can be a specialist. That means that, in addition to writing about schools and educational trends, our education reporter takes her turn filling in on the police beat, handling obituaries, writing lifestyle features, and even taking an occasional picture.

And because you are closer to your readers, small towns are great places for young journalists to learn the craft. Most of our regular sources and many readers realize the *Times-Gazette* is a training ground and that staff turnover is a fact of life. The mayor is amazingly patient in explaining the intricacies of the city's budget to yet another new reporter. That's one of the secrets about small-town journalism I have rediscovered.

The stories in smaller communities are just as good and compelling as those in a big city. And while we don't have the resources of bigger papers to go after those stories, sometimes we don't face the obstacles either. The level of journalism can be just as high.

My sales pitch to the folks I hire is: "I can't pay you lots of money, but give me two years and I can give you a range of experiences that will get you ready for bigger and better things."

I proudly tout that alumni of the *Times-Gazette* have worked in metro newspapers across the Midwest in addition to the *New York Times*, *USA TODAY*, the *Philadelphia Inquirer*, and *St. Petersburg Times*. In fact, former *T-G* staffer Kris Wells, who's spent most of the past twenty-five years in a variety of editing roles at the *New York Times*, was kind enough to come back and share with our staff first-hand about how he *Times-Gazette* was a great launching pad for her career.

One of the first questions former colleagues want to know is whether life at a small paper is any less hectic or stressful than at a metro. I tell them not really, but small-town life allows you to live daily life in smaller bites than in the big city. I can run home for lunch, or run over to my daughter's school for an activity and be back in the office within the hour. Or I can drop back by the office after supper for a few minutes to check things if need be. It's far easier to intersperse family life with work.

Sure, I occasionally still miss Indianapolis and *The Star*—especially the interaction with many wise and talented colleagues. But if I ever left the *T-G,* I'd miss the daily interactions with readers—especially when they come up and tell you, "Keep up the good work. You are making a difference." ✳

The future

Journalism, as it always has, is changing.

Now, though, change for everything comes faster than ever. To stay successful as a journalist, you have to change, too, and you'll have to grow even faster than you did while you were in school.

Hang up the learning and you'll hang up your career.

Any specifics I give you here about the new wrinkles, waves, and ways will be at least a little outdated by the time you read them.

I could tell you to explore digital journalism, to learn new ways of storytelling, and to pioneer new business models. We could start a new book. And it would all get outdated quickly.

So I am not going to give you specifics as I have in the rest of this book. Instead, I am going to leave you with one little story about a photojournalist who changed the way I manage my career. It helped me more than all the tips and bits of advice I have heard or gleaned along the way. I hope it helps you, too.

I was recruiting at the National Association of Black Journalists' convention and a veteran photographer asked me to critique his portfolio. He said he did not want a new job, but would appreciate some feedback. I began to look at the images. I told him that they were strong, clear, and varied.

"Thanks," he said, "I shot them all in the past year."

I stopped. "Wait. You tell me that you are not looking for a job, yet you have a fresh portfolio?"

"Yes. I always try to keep a fresh portfolio. I never want anything in there to be more than a year old. I always try to keep topping myself."

If you do like that photographer, if your ethic is to continually innovate, create, and stay current, if you do something every year that is good enough to make your résumé, you will be OK.

index

167

CPSIA information can be obtained
at www.ICGtesting.com
Printed in the USA
BVHW03s1638230518
517118BV00013B/190/P

9 781934 879030